MW00910931

S

THE SCIENCE OF GETTING RICH
and
THE PATH OF PROSPERITY

Part of the Inkstone Classics series

The Science of Getting Rich plus The Path of Prosperity
Copyright © 2007 Inkstone Press Pty Ltd, Australia

All rights reserved. No part of this publication may be reproduced,
stored in a retrieval system, or transmitted, in any form or by any means
without the prior written permission of the publisher, nor be otherwise
circulated in any form of binding or cover other than that in which it is
published and without a similar condition being imposed on the
subsequent purchaser.

ISBN: 978-0-9775792-1-1

Printed in Malaysia

THE SCIENCE
OF GETTING RICH
by Wallace C Wattles

————◆◆◆——— and ———◆◆◆———

THE PATH OF
PROSPERITY
by James Allen

THE SCIENCE OF GETTING RICH
Page 7

THE PATH OF PROSPERITY
Page 113

THE SCIENCE
OF GETTING
RICH

by
Wallace D. Wattles

CONTENTS

Chapter One

THE RIGHT TO BE RICH

WHATEVER may be said in praise of poverty, the fact remains that it is not possible to live a really complete or successful life unless one is rich. No man can rise to his greatest possible height in talent or soul development unless he has plenty of money; for to unfold the soul and to develop talent he must have many things to use, and he cannot have these things unless he has money to buy them with.

A man develops in mind, soul, and body by making use of things, and society is so organized that man must have money in order to become the possessor of things; therefore, the basis of all advancement for man must be the science of getting rich.

The object of all life is development; and everything that lives has an inalienable right to all the development it is capable of attaining.

Man's right to life means his right to have the free and unrestricted use of all the things which may be necessary to his fullest mental, spiritual, and physical unfoldment; or, in other words, his right to be rich.

In this book, I shall not speak of riches in a figurative way; to be really rich does not mean to be satisfied or contented with a little. No man ought to be satisfied with a little if he is capable of using and enjoying more. The purpose of Nature is the advancement and unfoldment of life; and every man should have all that can contribute to the power; elegance, beauty, and richness of life; to be content with less is sinful.

The man who owns all he wants for the living of all the life he is capable of living is rich; and no man who has not plenty of money can have all he wants. Life has advanced so far, and become so complex, that even the most ordinary man or woman requires a great amount of wealth in order to live in a manner that even approaches completeness. Every person naturally wants to become all that they are capable of becoming; this desire to realize innate possibilities is inherent in human nature; we cannot help wanting to be all that we can be. Success in life is becoming what you want to be; you can become what you want to be only by making use of things, and you can have the free use of things only as you become rich enough to buy them. To understand the science of getting rich is therefore the most essential of all knowledge.

There is nothing wrong in wanting to get rich. The desire for riches is really the desire for a richer, fuller, and more abundant life; and that desire is praise worthy. The man who does not desire to live more abundantly is abnormal, and so the man who does not desire to have money enough to buy all he wants is abnormal.

There are three motives for which we live; we live for the body, we live for the mind, we live for the soul. No one of these is better or holier than the other; all are alike desirable, and no one of the three—body, mind, or soul—can live fully if either of the others is cut short of full life and expression. It is not right or noble to live only for the soul and deny mind or body; and it is wrong to live for the intellect and deny body or soul.

We are all acquainted with the loathsome consequences of living for the body and denying both mind and soul; and we see that real life means the complete expression of all that man can give forth through body, mind, and soul. Whatever he can say, no man can be really happy or satisfied unless his body is living fully in every function, and unless the same is true of his mind and his soul. Wherever there is unexpressed possibility, or function not performed, there is unsatisfied desire. Desire is possibility seeking expression, or function seeking performance.

Man cannot live fully in body without good food, comfortable clothing, and warm shelter; and without freedom from excessive toil. Rest and recreation are also necessary to his physical life.

He cannot live fully in mind without books and time to study them, without opportunity for travel and observation, or without intellectual companionship.

To live fully in mind he must have intellectual recreations, and must surround himself with all the objects of art and beauty he is capable of using and appreciating.

To live fully in soul, man must have love; and love is denied expression by poverty.

A man's highest happiness is found in the bestowal of benefits on those he loves; love finds its most natural and spontaneous expression in giving. The man who has nothing to give cannot fill his place as a husband or father, as a citizen, or as a man. It is in the use of material things that a man finds full life for his body, develops his mind, and unfolds his soul. It is therefore of supreme importance to him that he should be rich.

It is perfectly right that you should desire to be rich; if you are a normal man or woman you cannot help doing so. It is perfectly right that you should give your best attention to the Science of Getting Rich, for it is the noblest and most necessary of all studies. If you neglect this study, you are derelict in your duty to yourself, to God and humanity; for you can render to God and humanity no greater service than to make the most of yourself.

Chapter Two

THERE IS A SCIENCE
OF GETTING RICH

THERE is a Science of getting rich, and it is an exact science, like algebra or arithmetic. There are certain laws which govern the process of acquiring riches; once these laws are learned and obeyed by any man, he will get rich with mathematical certainty.

The ownership of money and property comes as a result of doing things in a certain way; those who do things in this Certain Way, whether on purpose or accidentally, get rich; while those who do not do things in this Certain Way, no matter how hard they work or how able they are, remain poor.

It is a natural law that like causes always produce like effects; and, therefore, any man or woman who learns to do things in this certain way will infallibly get rich.

That the above statement is true is shown by the following facts:

Getting rich is not a matter of environment, for, if it were, all the people in certain neighborhoods would become wealthy;

the people of one city would all be rich, while those of other towns would all be poor; or the inhabitants of one state would roll in wealth, while those of an adjoining state would be in poverty.

But everywhere we see rich and poor living side by side, in the same environment, and often engaged in the same vocations. When two men are in the same locality, and in the same business, and one gets rich while the other remains poor, it shows that getting rich is not, primarily, a matter of environment. Some environments may be more favorable than others, but when two men in the same business are in the same neighborhood, and one gets rich while the other fails, it indicates that getting rich is the result of doing things in a Certain Way.

And further, the ability to do things in this certain way is not due solely to the possession of talent, for many people who have great talent remain poor, while other who have very little talent get rich.

Studying the people who have got rich, we find that they are an average lot in all respects, having no greater talents and abilities than other men. It is evident that they do not get rich because they possess talents and abilities that other men have not, but because they happen to do things in a Certain Way.

Getting rich is not the result of saving, or "thrift"; many very penurious people are poor, while free spenders often get rich.

Nor is getting rich due to doing things which others fail to do; for two men in the same business often do almost exactly the same things, and one gets rich while the other remains poor or becomes bankrupt.

From all these things, we must come to the conclusion that getting rich is the result of doing things in a Certain Way.

If getting rich is the result of doing things in a Certain Way, and if like causes always produce like effects, then any man or woman who can do things in that way can become rich, and the whole matter is brought within the domain of exact science.

The question arises here, whether this Certain Way may not be so difficult that only a few may follow it. This cannot be true, as we have seen, so far as natural ability is concerned. Talented people get rich, and blockheads get rich; intellectually brilliant people get rich, and very stupid people get rich; physically strong people get rich, and weak and sickly people get rich.

Some degree of ability to think and understand is, of course, essential; but in so far natural ability is concerned, any man or woman who has sense enough to read and understand these words can certainly get rich.

Also, we have seen that it is not a matter of environment. Location counts for something; one would not go to the heart of the Sahara and expect to do successful business.

Getting rich involves the necessity of dealing with men, and of being where there are people to deal with; and if these people are inclined to deal in the way you want to deal, so much the better. But that is about as far as environment goes.

If anybody else in your town can get rich, so can you; and if anybody else in your state can get rich, so can you.

Again, it is not a matter of choosing some particular business or profession. People get rich in every business, and in every profession; while their next door neighbors in the same vocation remain in poverty.

It is true that you will do best in a business which you like, and which is congenial to you; and if you have certain talents which are well developed, you will do best in a business which calls for the exercise of those talents.

Also, you will do best in a business which is suited to your locality; an ice-cream parlor would do better in a warm climate than in Greenland, and a salmon fishery will succeed better in the Northwest than in Florida, where there are no salmon.

But, aside from these general limitations, getting rich is not dependent upon your engaging in some particular business, but upon your learning to do things in a Certain Way. If you are now in business, and anybody else in your locality is getting rich in the same business, while you are not getting rich, it is because you are not doing things in the same Way that the other person is doing them.

No one is prevented from getting rich by lack of capital. True, as you get capital the increase becomes more easy and rapid; but one who has capital is already rich, and does not need to consider how to become so. No matter how poor you may be, if you begin to do things in the Certain Way you will begin to get rich; and you will begin to have capital. The getting of capital is a part of the process of getting rich; and it is a part of the result which invariably follows the doing of things in the Certain Way. You may be the poorest man on the continent, and be deeply in debt; you may have neither friends, influence, nor resources; but if you begin to do things in this way, you must infallibly begin to get rich, for like causes must produce like effects. If you have no capital, you can get capital; if you are in the wrong business, you can get into the right business; if you are in the wrong location, you can go to the right location; and you can do so *by beginning in your present business and in your present location* to do things in the Certain Way which causes success.

Chapter Three

IS OPPORTUNITY MONOPOLIZED

NO man is kept poor because opportunity has been taken away from him; because other people have monopolized the wealth, and have put a fence around it. You may be shut off from engaging in business in certain lines, but there are other channels open to you. Probably it would be hard for you to get control of any of the great railroad systems; that field is pretty well monopolized. But the electric railway business is still in its infancy, and offers plenty of scope for enterprise; and it will be but a very few years until traffic and transportation through the air will become a great industry, and in all its branches will give employment to hundreds of thousands, and perhaps to millions, of people. Why not turn your attention to the development of aerial transportation, instead of competing with J. J. Hill and others for a chance in the steam railway world?

It is quite true that if you are a workman in the employ of the steel trust you have very little chance of becoming the owner of the plant in which you work; but it is also true that if you will commence to act in a Certain Way, you can soon leave the employ of the steel trust; you can buy a farm of from ten to forty acres, and engage in business as a producer of foodstuffs. There is great opportunity at this time for men who will live upon small tracts of land and cultivate the same intensively; such men will certainly get rich. You may say that it is impossible for you to get the land, but I am going to prove to you that it is not impossible, and that you can certainly get a farm if you will go to work in a Certain Way.

At different periods the tide of opportunity sets in different directions, according to the needs of the whole, and the particular stage of social evolution which has been reached. At present, in America, it is setting toward agriculture and the allied industries and professions. Today, opportunity is open before the factory worker in his line. It is open before the business man who supplies the farmer more than before the one who supplies the factory worker; and before the professional man who waits upon the farmer more than before the one who serves the working class.

There is abundance of opportunity for the man who will go with the tide, instead of trying to swim against it.

So the factory workers, either as individuals or as a class, are not deprived of opportunity. The workers are not being "kept down" by their masters; they are not being "ground" by the trusts and combinations of capital. As a class, they are where they are because they do not do things in a Certain Way. If the workers of America chose to do so, they could follow the example of their brothers in Belgium and other countries, and establish great department stores and co-operative industries; they could elect men of their own class to office, and pass laws favoring the development of such co-operative industries; and in a few years they could take peaceable possession of the industrial field.

The working class may become the master class whenever they will begin to do things in a Certain Way; the law of wealth is the same for them as it is for all others. This they must learn; and they will remain where they are as long as they continue to do as they do. The individual worker, however, is not held down by the ignorance or the mental slothfulness of his class; he can follow the tide of opportunity to riches, and this book will tell him how.

No one is kept in poverty by a shortness in the supply of riches; there is more than enough for all. A palace as large as the capitol at Washington might be built for every family on earth from the building material in the United States alone; and under intensive cultivation, this country would produce wool, cotton, linen, and silk enough to cloth each person in the world finer than Solomon was arrayed in all his glory; together with food enough to feed them all luxuriously.

The visible supply is practically inexhaustible; and the invisible supply really *is* inexhaustible.

Everything you see on earth is made from one original substance, out of which all things proceed.

New Forms are constantly being made, and older ones are dissolving; but all are shapes assumed by One Thing.

There is no limit to the supply of Formless Stuff, or Original Substance. The universe is made out of it; but it was not all used in making the universe. The spaces in, through, and between the forms of the visible universe are permeated and filled with the Original Substance; with the formless Stuff; with the raw material of all things. Ten thousand times as much as has been made might still be made, and even then we should not have exhausted the supply of universal raw material.

No man, therefore, is poor because nature is poor, or because there is not enough to go around.

Nature is an inexhaustible storehouse of riches; the supply will never run short. Original Substance is alive with creative energy, and is constantly producing more forms. When the supply of building material is exhausted, more will be produced; when the soil is exhausted so that food stuffs and materials for clothing will no longer grow upon it, it will be renewed or more soil will be made. When all the gold and silver has been dug from the earth, if man is still in such a stage of social development that he needs gold and silver, more will produced from the Formless. The Formless Stuff responds to the needs of man; it will not let him be without any good thing.

This is true of man collectively; the race as a whole is always abundantly rich, and if individuals are poor, it is because they do not follow the Certain Way of doing things which makes the individual man rich.

The Formless Stuff is intelligent; it is stuff which thinks. It is alive, and is always impelled toward more life.

It is the natural and inherent impulse of life to seek to live more; it is the nature of intelligence to enlarge itself, and of consciousness to seek to extend its boundaries and find fuller expression. The universe of forms has been made by Formless Living Substance, throwing itself into form in order to express itself more fully.

The universe is a great Living Presence, always moving inherently toward more life and fuller functioning.

Nature is formed for the advancement of life; its impelling motive is the increase of life. For this cause, everything which can possibly minister to life is bountifully provided; there can be no lack unless God is to contradict himself and nullify his own works.

You are not kept poor by lack in the supply of riches; it is a fact which I shall demonstrate a little farther on that even the resources of the Formless Supply are at the command of the man or woman will act and think in a Certain Way.

Chapter Four

THE FIRST PRINCIPLE IN THE SCIENCE OF GETTING RICH

THOUGHT is the only power which can produce tangible riches from the Formless Substance. The stuff from which all things are made is a substance which thinks, and a thought of form in this substance produces the form.

Original Substance moves according to its thoughts; every form and process you see in nature is the visible expression of a thought in Original Substance. As the Formless Stuff thinks of a form, it takes that form; as it thinks of a motion, it makes that motion. That is the way all things were created. We live in a thought world, which is part of a thought universe. The thought of a moving universe extended throughout Formless Substance, and the Thinking Stuff moving according to that thought, took the form of systems of planets, and maintains that form. Thinking Substance takes the form of its thought, and moves according to the thought. Holding the idea of a circling system of suns and worlds, it takes the form of these bodies, and moves them as it thinks. Thinking the form of a slow-growing oak tree, it moves accordingly, and produces the tree, though centuries may be required to do the work. In creating, the Formless seems to move according to the lines of motion it has established; the thought of an oak tree does not cause the instant formation of a full-grown tree, but it does start in motion the forces which will produce the tree, along established lines of growth.

Every thought of form, held in thinking Substance, causes the creation of the form, but always, or at least generally, along lines of growth and action already established.

The thought of a house of a certain construction, if it were impressed upon Formless Substance, might not cause the instant formation, of the house; but it would cause the turning of creative energies already working in trade and commerce into such channels as to result in the speedy building of the house. And if there were no existing channels through which the creative energy could work, then the house would be formed directly from primal substance, without waiting for the slow processes of the organic and inorganic world.

No thought of form can be impressed upon Original Substance without causing the creation of the form.

Man is a thinking center, and can originate thought. All the forms that man fashions with his hands must first exist in his thought; he cannot shape a thing until he has thought that thing.

And so far man has confined his efforts wholly to the work of his hands; he has applied manual labor to the world of forms, seeking to change or modify those already existing. He has never thought of trying to cause the creation of new forms by impressing his thoughts upon Formless Substance. *Faith*

When man has a thought-force, he takes material from the forms of nature, and makes an image of the form which is in his mind. He has, so far, made little or no effort to co-operate with Formless Intelligence; to work "with the Father." He has not dreamed that he can "do what he Seth the Father doing." Man reshapes and modifies existing forms by manual labor; he has given no attention to the question whether he may not produce things from Formless Substance by communicating his thoughts to it. We propose to prove that he may do so; to prove that any man or woman may do so, and to show how. As our first step, we must lay down three fundamental propositions.

First, we assert that there is one original formless stuff, or substance, from which all things are made. All the seemingly many elements are but different presentations of one element; all the many forms found in organic and inorganic nature are but different shapes, made from the same stuff. And this stuff is thinking stuff; a thought held in it produces the form of the thought. Thought, in thinking substance, produces shapes. Man is a thinking center, capable of original thought; if man can communicate his thought to original thinking substance, he can cause the creation, or formation, of the thing he thinks about. To summarize this:—

There is a thinking stuff from which all things are made, and which, in its original state, permeates, penetrates, and fills the interstices of the universe.

A thought, in this substance, Produces the thing that is imaged by the thought.

Man can form things in his thought, and, by impressing his thought upon formless substance, can cause the thing he thinks about to be created.

It may be asked if I can prove these statements; and without going into details, I answer that I can do so, both by logic and experience.

Reasoning back from the phenomena of form and thought, I come to one original thinking substance; and reasoning forward from this thinking substance, I come to man's power to cause the formation of the thing he thinks about.

And by experiment, I find the reasoning true; and this is my strongest proof.

If one man who reads this book gets rich by doing what it tells him to do, that is evidence in support of my claim; but if every man who does what it tells him to do gets rich, that is positive proof until some one goes through the process and fails. The theory is true until the process fails; and this process will not fail, for every man who does exactly what this book tells him to do will get rich.

I have said that men get rich by doing things in a Certain Way; and in order to do so, men must become able to think in a certain way.

A man's way of doing things is the direct result of the way he thinks about things.

To do things in a way you want to do them, you will have to acquire the ability to think the way you want to think; this is the first step toward getting rich.

To think what you want to think is to think TRUTH, regardless of appearances.

Every man has the natural and inherent power to think what he wants to think, but it requires far more effort to do so than it does to think the thoughts which are suggested by appearances. To think according to appearance is easy; to think truth regardless of appearances is laborious, and requires the expenditure of more power than any other work man is called upon to perform.

There is no labor from which most people shrink as they do from that of sustained and consecutive thought; it is the hardest work in the world. This is especially true when truth is contrary to appearances. Every appearance in the visible world tends to produce a corresponding form in the mind which observes it; and this can only be prevented by holding the thought of the TRUTH. *GOD's Word.*

To look upon the appearance of disease will produce the form of disease in your own mind, and ultimately in your body, unless you hold the thought of the truth, which is that there is no disease; it is only an appearance, and the reality is health.

To look upon the appearances of poverty will produce corresponding forms in your own mind, unless you hold to the truth that there is no poverty; there is only abundance. *Create it in your mind.*

To think health when surrounded by the appearances of disease, or to think riches when in the midst of appearances of poverty, requires power; but he who acquires this power becomes a MASTER MIND. He can conquer fate; he can have what he wants.

This power can only be acquired by getting hold of the basic fact which is behind all appearances; and that fact is that there is one Thinking Substance, from which and by which all things are made. *GOD's word.*

Then we must grasp the truth that every thought held in this substance becomes a form, and that man can so impress his thoughts upon it as to cause them to take form and become visible things.

When we realize this, we lose all doubt and fear, for we know that we can create what we want to create; we can get what we want to have, and can become what we want to be. As a first step toward getting rich, you must believe the three fundamental statements given previously in this chapter; and in order to emphasize them. I repeat them here:-

There is a thinking stuff from which all things are made, and which, in its original state, permeates, penetrates, and fills the interspaces of the universe.

A thought, in this substance, Produces the thing that is imaged by the thought.

Man can form things in his thought, and, by impressing his thought upon formless substance, can cause the thing he thinks about to be created. Faith .

You must lay aside all other concepts of the universe than this monistic one; and you must dwell upon this until it is fixed in your mind, and has become your habitual thought. Read these creed statements over and over again; fix every word upon your memory, and meditate upon them until you firmly believe what they say. If a doubt comes to you, cast it aside as a sin. Do not listen to arguments against this idea; do not go to churches or lectures where a contrary concept of things is taught or preached. Do not read magazines or books which teach a different idea; if you get mixed up in your faith, all your efforts will be in vain.

Do not ask why these things are true, nor speculate as to how they can be true; simply take them on trust.

The science of getting rich begins with the absolute acceptance of this faith.

Chapter Five

INCREASING LIFE

YOU must get rid of the last vestige of the old idea that there is a Deity whose will it is that you should be poor, or whose purposes may be served by keeping you in poverty.

The Intelligent Substance which is All, and in All, and which lives in All and lives in you, is a consciously Living Substance. Being a consciously living substance, It must have the nature and inherent desire of every living intelligence for increase of life. Every living thing must continually seek for the enlargement of its life, because life, in the mere act of living, must increase itself.

A seed, dropped into the ground, springs into activity, and in the act of living produces a hundred more seeds; life, by living, multiplies itself. It is forever Becoming More; it must do so, if it continues to be at all.

Intelligence is under this same necessity for continuous increase. Every thought we think makes it necessary for us to think another thought; consciousness is continually expanding. Every fact we learn leads us to the learning of another fact; knowledge is continually increasing. Every talent we cultivate brings to the mind the desire to cultivate another talent; we are subject to the urge of life, seeking expression, which ever drives us on to know more, to do more, and to be more.

In order to know more, do more, and be more we must have more; we must have things to use, for we learn, and do, and become, only by using things. We must get rich, so that we can live more.

The desire for riches is simply the capacity for larger life seeking fulfillment; every desire is the effort of an unexpressed possibility to come into action. It is power seeking to manifest which causes desire. That which makes you want more money is the same as that which makes the plant grow; it is Life, seeking fuller expression.

The One Living Substance must be subject to this inherent law of all life; it is permeated with the desire to live more; that is why it is under the necessity of creating things.

The One Substance desires to live more in you; hence it wants you to have all the things you can use.

It is the desire of God that you should get rich. He wants you to get rich because he can express himself better through you if you have plenty of things to use in giving him expression. He can live more in you if you have unlimited command of the means of life.

The universe desires you to have everything you want to have.

Nature is friendly to your plans.

Everything is naturally for you.

Make up your mind that this is true.

It is essential, however that *your purpose should harmonize with the purpose that is in All.*

You must want real life, not mere pleasure of sensual gratification. Life is the performance of function; and the individual really lives only when he performs every function, physical, mental, and spiritual, of which he is capable, without excess in any.

You do not want to get rich in order to live swinishly, for the gratification of animal desires; that is not life. But the performance of every physical function is a part of life, and no one lives completely who denies the impulses of the body a normal and healthful expression.

You do not want to get rich solely to enjoy mental pleasures, to get knowledge, to gratify ambition, to outshine others, to be famous. All these are a legitimate part of life, but the man who lives for the pleasures of the intellect alone will only have a partial life, and he will never be satisfied with his lot.

You do not want to get rich solely for the good of others, to lose yourself for the salvation of mankind, to experience the joys of philanthropy and sacrifice. The joys of the soul are only a part of life; and they are no better or nobler than any other part.

You want to get rich in order that you may eat, drink, and be merry when it is time to do these things; in order that you may surround yourself with beautiful things, see distant lands, feed your mind, and develop your intellect; in order that you may love men and do kind things, and be able to play a good part in helping the world to find truth.

But remember that extreme altruism is no better and no nobler than extreme selfishness; both are mistakes.

Get rid of the idea that God wants you to sacrifice yourself for others, and that you can secure his favor by doing so; God requires nothing of the kind.

What he wants is that you should make the most of yourself, for yourself, and for others; and *you can help others more by making the most of yourself than in any other way.*

You can make the most of yourself only by getting rich; so it is right and praiseworthy that you should give your first and best thought to the work of acquiring wealth.

Remember, however, that the desire of Substance is for all, and its movements must be for more life to all; it cannot be made to work for less life to any, because it is equally in all, seeking riches and life.

Intelligent Substance will make things for you, but it will not take things away from some one else and give them to you.

You must get rid of the thought of competition. You are to create, not to compete for what is already created.

You do not have to take anything away from anyone.

You do not have to drive sharp bargains.

You do not have to cheat, or to take advantage. You do not need to let any man work for you for less than he earns.

You do not have to covet the property of others, or to look at it with wishful eyes; no man has anything of which you cannot have the like, and that without taking what he has away from him.

You are to become a creator, not a competitor; you are going to get what you want, but in such a way that when you get it every other man will have more than he has now.

I am aware that there are men who get a vast amount of money by proceeding in direct opposition to the statements in the paragraph above, and may add a word of explanation here. Men of the plutocratic type, who become very rich, do so sometimes purely by their extraordinary ability on the plane of competition; and sometimes they unconsciously relate themselves to Substance in its great purposes and movements for the general racial upbuilding through industrial evolution. Rockefeller, Carnegie, Morgan, et al., have been the unconscious agents of the Supreme in the necessary work of systematizing and organizing productive industry; and in the end, their work will contribute immensely toward increased life for all. Their day is nearly over; they have organized production, *and will soon be succeeded by the agents of the multitude, who will organize the machinery of distribution.*

The multi-millionaires are like the monster reptiles of the prehistoric eras; they play a necessary part in the evolutionary process, but the same Power which produced them will dispose of them. And it is well to bear in mind that they have never been really rich; a record of the private lives of most of this class will show that they have really been the most abject and wretched of the poor.

Riches secured on the competitive plane are never satisfactory and permanent; they are yours today, and another's tomorrow. Remember, if you are to become rich in a scientific and certain way, you must rise entirely out of the competitive thought. You must never think for a moment that the supply is limited. Just as soon as you begin to think that all the money is being "cornered" and controlled by bankers and others, and that you must exert yourself to get laws passed to stop this process, and so on; in that moment you drop into the competitive mind, and your power to cause creation is gone for the time being; and what is worse, you will probably arrest the creative movements you have already instituted.

 KNOW that there are countless millions of dollars' worth of gold in the mountains of the earth, not yet brought to light; and know that if there were not, more would be created from Thinking Substance to supply your needs.

 KNOW that the money you need will come, even if it is necessary for a thousand men to be led to the discovery of new gold mines to-morrow.

Never look at the visible supply; look always at the limitless riches in Formless Substance, and KNOW that they are coming to you as fast as you can receive and use them. Nobody, by cornering the visible supply, can prevent you from getting what is yours.

So never allow yourself to think for an instant that all the best building spots will be taken before you get ready to build your house, unless you hurry. Never worry about the trusts and combines, and get anxious for fear they will soon come to own the whole earth. Never get afraid that you will lose what you want because some other person "beats you to it." That cannot possibly happen; you are not seeking any thing that is possessed by anybody else; you are causing what you want to be created from formless Substance, and the supply is without limits. Stick to the formulated statement:—

There is a thinking stuff from which all things are made, and which, in its original state, permeates, penetrates, and fills the interspaces of the universe.

A thought, in this substance, produces the thing that is imaged by the thought.

Man can form things in his thought, and, by impressing his thought upon formless substance, can cause the thing he thinks about to be created.

Chapter Six

HOW RICHES COME TO YOU

WHEN I say that you do not have to drive sharp bargains, I do not mean that you do not have to drive any bargains at all, or that you are above the necessity for having any dealings with your fellow men. I mean that you will not need to deal with them unfairly; you do not have to get something for nothing, *but can give to every man more than you take from him.*

You cannot give every man more in cash market value than you take from him, but you can give him more in use value than the cash value of the thing you take from him. The paper, ink, and other material in this book may not be worth the money you pay for it; but if the ideas suggested by it bring you thousands of dollars, you have not been wronged by those who sold it to you; they have given you a great use value for a small cash value.

Let us suppose that I own a picture by one of the great artists, which, in any civilized community, is worth thousands of dollars. I take it to Baffin Ray, and by "salesmanship" induce an Eskimo to give a bundle of furs worth $500 for it. I have really wronged him, for he has no use for the picture; it has no use value to him; it will not add to his life.

But suppose I give him a gun worth $50 for his furs; then he has made a good bargain. He has use for the gun; it will get him many more furs and much food; it will add to his life in every way; it will make him rich.

When you rise from the competitive to the creative plane, you can scan your business transactions very strictly, and if you are selling any man anything which does not add more to his life than the thing he give you in exchange, you can afford to stop it. You do not have to beat anybody in business. And if you are in a business which does beat people, get out of it at once.

Give every man more in use value than you take from him in cash value; then you are adding to the life of the world by every business transaction.

If you have people working for you, you must take from them more in cash value than you pay them in wages; but you can so organize your business that it will be filled with the principle of advancement, and so that each employee who wishes to do so may advance a little every day.

You can make your business do for your employees what this book is doing for you. You can so conduct your business that it will be a sort of ladder, by which every employee who will take the trouble may climb to riches himself; and given the opportunity, if he will not do so it is not your fault.

And finally, because you are to cause the creation of your riches from Formless Substance which permeates all your environment, it does not follow that they are to take shape from the atmosphere and come into being before your eyes.

If you want a sewing machine, for instance, I do not mean to tell you that you are to impress the thought of a sewing machine on Thinking Substance until the machine is formed without hands, in the room where you sit, or elsewhere. But if you want a sewing machine, hold the mental image of it with the most positive certainty that it is being made, or is on its way to you. After once forming the thought, have the most absolute and unquestioning faith that the sewing machine is coming; never think of it, or speak, of it, in any other way than as being sure to arrive. Claim it as already yours.

It will be brought to you by the power of the Supreme Intelligence, acting upon the minds of men. If you live in Maine, it may be that a man will be brought from Texas or Japan to engage in some transaction which will result in your getting what you want.

If so, the whole matter will be as much to that man's advantage as it is to yours.

Do not forget for a moment that the Thinking Substance is through all, in all, communicating with all, and can influence all. The desire of Thinking Substance for fuller life and better living has caused the creation of all the sewing machines already made; and it can cause the creation of millions more, and will, whenever men set it in motion by desire and faith, and by acting in a Certain Way.

You can certainly have a sewing machine in your house; and it is just as certain that you can have any other thing or things which you want, and which you will use for the advancement of your own life and the lives of others.

You need not hesitate about asking largely; "it is your Father's pleasure to give you the kingdom, " said Jesus.

Original Substance wants to live all that is possible in you, and wants you to have all that you can or will use for the living of the most abundant life.

If you fix upon your consciousness the fact that the desire you feel for the possession of riches is one with the desire of Omnipotence for more complete expression, your faith becomes invincible.

Once I saw a little boy sitting at a piano, and vainly trying to bring harmony out of the keys; and I saw that he was grieved and provoked by his inability to play real music. I asked him the cause of his vexation, and he answered, "I can feel the music in me, but I can't make my hands go right." The music in him was the URGE of Original Substance, containing all the possibilities of all life; all that there is of music was seeking expression through the child.

God, the One Substance, is trying to live and do and enjoy things through humanity. He is saying "I want hands to build wonderful structures, to play divine harmonies, to paint glorious pictures; I want feet to run my errands, eyes to see my beauties, tongues to tell mighty truths and to sing marvelous songs," and so on.

All that there is of possibility is seeking expression through men. God wants those who can play music to have pianos and every other instrument, and to have the means to cultivate their talents to the fullest extent; He wants those who can appreciate beauty to be able to surround themselves with beautiful things; He wants those who can discern truth to have every opportunity to travel and observe; He wants those who can appreciate dress to be beautifully clothed, and those who can appreciate good food to be luxuriously fed.

He wants all these things because it is Himself that enjoys and appreciates them; it is God who wants to play, and sing, and enjoy beauty, and proclaim truth and wear fine clothes, and eat good foods. "it is God that worketh in you to will and to do," said Paul.

The desire you feel for riches is the infinite, seeking to express Himself in you as He sought to find expression in the little boy at the piano.

So you need not hesitate to ask largely.

Your part is to focalize and express the desire to God.

This is a difficult point with most people; they retain something of the old idea that poverty and self-sacrifice are pleasing to God. They look upon poverty as a part of the plan, a necessity of nature. They have the idea that God has finished His work, and made all that He can make, and that the majority of men must stay poor because there is not enough to go around. They hold to so much of this erroneous thought that they feel ashamed to ask for wealth; they try not to want more than a very modest competence, just enough to make them fairly comfortable.

I recall now the case of one student who was told that he must get in mind a clear picture of the things he desired, so that the creative thought of them might be impressed on Formless Substance. He was a very poor man, living in a rented house, and having only what he earned from day to day; and he could not grasp the fact that all wealth was his. So, after thinking the matter over, he decided that he might reasonably ask for a new rug for the floor of his best room, and an anthracite coal stove to heat the house during the cold weather. Following the instructions given in this book, he obtained these things in a few months; and then it dawned upon him that he had not asked enough. He went through the house in which he lived, and planned all the improvements he would like to make in it; he mentally added a bay window here and a room there, until it was complete in his mind as his ideal home; and then he planned its furnishings.

Holding the whole picture in his mind, he began living in the Certain Way, and moving toward what he wanted; and he owns the house now, and is rebuilding it after the form of his mental image. And now, with still larger faith, he is going on to get greater things. It has been unto him according to his faith, and it is so with you and with all of us.

Chapter Seven

GRATITUDE

THE illustrations given in the last chapter will have conveyed to the reader the fact that the first step toward getting rich is to convey the idea of your wants to the Formless Substance.

This is true, and you will see that in order to do so it becomes necessary to relate yourself to the Formless Intelligence in a harmonious way.

To secure this harmonious relation is a matter of such primary and vital importance that I shall give some space to its discussion here, and give you instructions which, if you will follow them, will be certain to bring you into perfect unity of mind with God.

The whole process of mental adjustment and atonement can be summed up in one word, gratitude.

First, you believe that there is one Intelligent Substance, from which all things proceed; second, you believe that this Substance gives you everything you desire; and third, you relate yourself to it by a feeling of deep and profound gratitude.

Many people who order their lives rightly in all other ways are kept in poverty by their lack of gratitude. Having received one gift from God, they cut the wires which connect them with Him by failing to make acknowledgment.

It is easy to understand that the nearer we live to the source of wealth, the more wealth we shall receive; and it is easy also to understand that the soul that is always grateful lives in closer touch with God than the one which never looks to Him in thankful acknowledgment.

The more gratefully we fix our minds on the Supreme when good things come to us, the more good things we will receive, and the more rapidly they will come; and the reason simply is that the mental attitude of gratitude draws the mind into closer touch with the source from which the blessings come.

If it is a new thought to you that gratitude brings your whole mind into closer harmony with the creative energies of the universe, consider it well, and you will see that it is true. The good things you already have have come to you along the line of obedience to certain laws. Gratitude will lead your mind out along the ways by which things come; and it will keep you in close harmony with creative thought and prevent you from falling into competitive thought.

Gratitude alone can keep you looking toward the All, and prevent you from falling into the error of thinking of the supply as limited; and to do that would be fatal to your hopes.

There is a Law of Gratitude, and it is absolutely necessary that you should observe the law, if you are to get the results you seek.

The law of gratitude is the natural principle that action and reaction are always equal, and in opposite directions.

The grateful outreaching of your mind in thankful praise to the Supreme *is a liberation or expenditure of force; it cannot fail to reach that to which it addressed, and the reaction is an instantaneous movement towards you.*

"Draw nigh unto God, and He will draw nigh unto you." That is a statement of psychological truth.

And if your gratitude is strong and constant, the reaction in Formless Substance will be strong and continuous; the movement of the things you want will be always toward you. Notice the grateful attitude that Jesus took; how He always seems to be saying, "I thank Thee, Father, that Thou hearest me." You cannot exercise much power without gratitude; for it is gratitude that keeps you connected with Power.

But the value of gratitude does not consist solely in getting you more blessings in the future. Without gratitude you cannot long keep from dissatisfied thought regarding things as they are.

The moment you permit your mind to dwell with dissatisfaction upon things as they are, you begin to lose ground. You fix attention upon the common, the ordinary, the poor, and the squalid and mean; and your mind takes the form of these things. Then you will transmit these forms or mental images to the Formless, and the common, the poor, the squalid, and mean will come to you.

To permit your mind to dwell upon the inferior is to become inferior and to surround yourself with inferior things.

On the other hand, to fix your attention on the best is to surround yourself with the best, and to become the best.

The Creative Power within us makes us into the image of that to which we give our attention. *(Don't talk about what you don't have)*

We are Thinking Substance, and thinking substance always takes the form of that which it thinks about.

The grateful mind is constantly fixed upon the best; therefore it tends to become the best; it takes the form or character of the best, and will receive the best.

Also, faith is born of gratitude. The grateful mind continually expects good things, and expectation becomes faith. The reaction of gratitude upon one's own mind produces faith; and every outgoing wave of grateful thanksgiving increases faith. He who has no feeling of gratitude cannot long retain a living faith; and without a living faith you cannot get rich by

Expectation invokes attraction.
Never desire something w/o expecting it.

the creative method, as we shall see in the following chapters.

It is necessary, then, to cultivate the habit of being grateful for every good thing that comes to you; and to give thanks continuously.

And because all things have contributed to your advancement, you should include all things in your gratitude.

Do not waste time thinking or talking about the shortcomings or wrong actions of plutocrats or trust magnates. Their organization of the world has made your opportunity; all you get really comes to you because of them.

Do not rage against, corrupt politicians; if it were not for politicians we should fall into anarchy, and your opportunity would be greatly lessened.

God has worked a long time and very patiently to bring us up to where we are in industry and government, and He is going right on with His work. There is not the least doubt that He will do away with plutocrats, trust magnates, captains of industry, and politicians as soon as they can be spared; but in the meantime, behold they are all very good. Remember that they are all helping to arrange the lines of transmission along which your riches will come to you, and be grateful to them all. This will bring you into harmonious relations with the good in everything, and the good in everything will move toward you.

Chapter Eight

THINKING IN THE CERTAIN WAY

TURN back to chapter 6 and read again the story of the man who formed a mental image of his house, and you will get a fair idea of the initial step toward getting rich. You must form a clear and definite mental picture of what you want; you cannot transmit an idea unless you have it yourself.

You must have it before you can give it; and many people fail to impress Thinking Substance because they have themselves only a vague and misty concept of the things they want to do, to have, or to become.

It is not enough that you should have a general desire for wealth "to do good with"; everybody has that desire.

It is not enough that you should have a wish to travel, see things, live more, etc. Everybody has those desires also. If you were going to send a wireless message to a friend, you would not send the letters of the alphabet in their order, and let him construct the message for himself; nor would you take words at random from the dictionary. You would send a coherent sentence; one which meant something. When you try to impress your wants upon Substance, remember that it must be done by a coherent statement; you must know what you want, and be definite. You can never get rich, or start the creative power into action, by sending out unformed longings and vague desires.

Go over your desires just as the man I have described went over his house; see just what you want, and get a clear mental picture of it as you wish it to look when you get it.

That clear mental picture you must have continually in mind, as the sailor has in mind the port toward which he is sailing the ship; you must keep your face toward it all the time. You must no more lose sight of it than the steersman loses sight of the compass.

It is not necessary to take exercises in concentration, nor to set apart special times for prayer and affirmation, nor to "go into the silence," nor to do occult stunts of any kind. There things are well enough, but all you need is to know what you want, and to want it badly enough so that it will stay in your thoughts.

Spend as much of your leisure time as you can in contemplating your picture, but no one needs to take exercises to concentrate his mind on a thing which he really wants; it is the things you do not really care about which require effort to fix your attention upon them.

And unless you really want to get rich, so that the desire is strong enough to hold your thoughts directed to the purpose as the magnetic pole holds the needle of the compass, it will hardly be worth while for you to try to carry out the instructions given in this book. *You have to want it. Why?*

The methods herein set forth are for people whose desire for riches is strong enough to overcome mental laziness and the love of ease, and make them work.

The more clear and definite you make your picture then, and the more you dwell upon it, bringing out all its delightful details, the stronger your desire will be; and the stronger your desire, the easier it will be to hold your mind fixed upon the picture of what you want.

Something more is necessary, however, than merely to see the picture clearly. If that is all you do, you are only a dreamer, and will have little or no power for accomplishment.

Behind your clear vision must be the purpose to realize it; to bring it out in tangible expression.

And behind this purpose must be an invincible and unwavering FAITH that the thing is already yours; that it is "at hand" and you have only to take possession of it.

Live in the new house, mentally, until it takes form around you physically. In the mental realm, enter at once into full enjoyment of the things you want.

"Whatsoever things ye ask for when ye pray, believe that ye receive them, and ye shall have them," said Jesus.

See the things you want as if they were actually around you all the time; see yourself as owning and using them. Make use of them in imagination just as you will use them when they are your tangible possessions. Dwell upon your mental picture until it is clear and distinct, and then take the Mental Attitude of Ownership toward everything in that picture. Take possession of it, in mind, in the full faith that it is actually yours. Hold to this mental ownership; do not waiver for an instant in the faith that it is real.

And remember what was said in a proceeding chapter about gratitude; be as thankful for it all the time as you expect to be <u>when it has taken form</u>. The man who can sincerely thank God for the things which as yet he owns only in imagination, has real faith. He will get rich; he will cause the creation of whatsoever he wants. *Be grateful when you ask for it*

You do not need to pray repeatedly for things you want; it is not necessary to tell God about it every day.

"Use not vain repetitions as the heathen do," said Jesus said to his pupils, "for your Father knoweth the ye have need of these things before ye ask Him."

Your part is to intelligently formulate your desire for the things which make for a larger life, and to get these desire arranged into a coherent whole; and then to impress this

Whole Desire upon the Formless Substance, which has the power and the will to bring you what you want.

You do not make this impression by repeating strings of words; you make it by holding the vision with unshakable PURPOSE to attain it, and with steadfast FAITH that you do attain it. *See what is- you have created the image.*

The answer to prayer is not according to your faith while you are talking, but according to your faith while you are working.

You cannot impress the mind of God by having a special Sabbath day set apart to tell Him what you want, and the forgetting Him during the rest of the week. You cannot impress Him by having special hours to go into your closet and pray, if you then dismiss the matter from your mind until the hour of prayer comes again.

Oral prayer is well enough, and has its effect, especially upon yourself, in clarifying your vision and strengthening your faith; but it is not your oral petitions which get you what you want. In order to get rich you do not need a "sweet hour of prayer"; you need to "pray without ceasing." And by prayer I mean holding steadily to your vision, with the purpose to cause its creation into solid form, and the faith that you are doing so.

"Believe that ye receive them."

The whole matter turns on receiving, once you have clearly formed your vision. When you have formed it, it is well to make an oral statement, addressing the Supreme in reverent prayer; and from that moment you must, in mind, receive what you ask for. Live in the new house; wear the fine clothes; ride in the automobile; go on the journey, and confidently plan for greater journeys. Think and speak of all the things you have asked for in terms of actual present ownership. Imagine an environment, and a financial condition exactly as you want them, and live all the time in that imaginary environment and financial condition. Mind, however, that you do not do this as a mere dreamer and castle builder; hold to the FAITH that the imaginary is being realized, and to the PURPOSE to realize it. Remember that it is faith and purpose in the use of the imagination which make the difference between the scientist and the dreamer. And having learned this fact, it is here that you must learn the proper use of the Will.

Chapter Nine

HOW TO USE YOUR WILL

⌐ what gives you mental strength

TO set about getting rich in a scientific way, you do not try to apply your will power to anything outside of yourself.

Your have no right to do so, anyway.

It is wrong to apply your will to other men and women, in order to get them to do what you wish done.

It is as flagrantly wrong to coerce people by mental power as it is to coerce them by physical power. If compelling people by physical force to do things for you reduces them to slavery, compelling them by mental means accomplishes exactly the same thing; the only difference is in methods. If taking things from people by physical force is robbery, them taking things by mental force is robbery also; there is no difference in principle.

You have no right to use your will power upon another person, even "for his own good"; for you do not know what is for his good. The science of getting rich does not require you to apply power or force to any other person, in any way whatsoever. There is not the slightest necessity for doing so;

indeed, any attempt to use your will upon others will only tend to defeat your purpose.

You do not need to apply your will to things, in order to compel them to come to you.

That would simply be trying to coerce God, and would be foolish and useless, as well as irreverent.

You do not have to compel God to give you good things, any more than you have to use your will power to make the sun rise.

You do not have to use your will power to conquer an unfriendly deity, or to make stubborn and rebellious forces do your bidding.

Substance is friendly to you, and is more anxious to give you what you want than you are to get it.

To get rich, you need only to use your will power upon yourself.

When you know what to think and do, then you must use your will to compel yourself to think and do the right things. That is the legitimate use of the will in getting what you want—to use it in holding yourself to the right course. Use your will to keep yourself thinking and acting in the Certain Way.

Do not try to project your will, or your thoughts, or your mind out into space, to "act" on things or people.

Keep your mind at home; it can accomplish more there than elsewhere.

Use your mind to form a mental image of what you want, and to hold that vision with faith and purpose; and use your will to keep your mind working in the Right Way.

The more steady and continuous your faith and purpose, the more rapidly you will get rich, because you will make only POSITIVE impressions upon Substance; and you will not neutralize or offset them by negative impressions.

The picture of your desires, held with faith and purpose, is taken up by the Formless, and permeates it to great distances-throughout the universe, for all I know.

As this impression spreads, all things are set moving toward its realization; every living thing, every inanimate thing, and the things yet uncreated, are stirred toward bringing into being that which you want. All force begins to be exerted in that direction; all things begin to move toward you. The minds of people, everywhere, are influenced toward doing the things necessary to the fulfilling of your desires; and they work for you, unconsciously.

But you can check all this by starting a negative impression in the Formless Substance. Doubt or unbelief is as certain to

Every thing we feared, happened.

start a movement away from you as faith and purpose are to start one toward you. It is by not understanding this that most people who try to make use of "mental science" in getting rich make their failure. Every hour and moment you spend in giving heed to doubts and fears, every hour you spend in worry, every hour in which your soul is possessed by unbelief, sets a current away from you in the whole domain of intelligent Substance. All the promises are unto them that believe, and unto them only. Notice how insistent Jesus was upon this point of belief; and now you know the reason why.

Since belief is all important, it behooves you to guard your thoughts; and as your beliefs will be shaped to a very great extent by the things you observe and think about, it is important that you should command your attention.

And here the will comes into use; for it is by your will that you determine upon what things your attention shall be fixed.

If you want to become rich, you must not make a study of poverty.

Things are not brought into being by thinking about their opposites. Health is never to be attained by studying disease and thinking about disease; righteousness is not to be promoted by studying sin and thinking about sin; and no one ever got rich by studying poverty and thinking about poverty.

Medicine as a science of disease has increased disease; religion as a science of sin has promoted sin, and economics as a study of poverty will fill the world with wretchedness and want.

Do not talk about poverty; do not investigate it, or concern yourself with it. Never mind what its causes are; you have nothing to do with them.

What concerns you is the cure.

Do not spend your time in charitable work, or charity movements; all charity only tends to perpetuate the wretchedness it aims to eradicate. *Educate people.*

I do not say that you should be hard hearted or unkind, and refuse to hear the cry of need; but you must not try to eradicate poverty in any of the conventional ways. Put poverty behind you, and put all that pertains to it behind you, and "make good."

Get rich; that is the best way you can help the poor.

And you cannot hold the mental image which is to make you rich if you fill your mind with pictures of poverty. Do not read books or papers which give circumstantial accounts of the wretchedness of the tenement dwellers, of the horrors of child labor, and so on. Do not read anything which fills your mind with gloomy images of want and suffering.

You cannot help the poor in the least by knowing about these things; and the wide-spread knowledge of them does not tend at all to do away with poverty.

What tends to do away with poverty is not the getting of pictures of poverty into your mind, but getting pictures of wealth into the minds of the poor.

You are not deserting the poor in their misery when you refuse to allow your mind to be filled with pictures of that misery.

Poverty can be done away with, not by increasing the number of well to do people who think about poverty, but by increasing the number of poor people who purpose with faith to get rich.

The poor do not need charity; they need inspiration. Charity only sends them a loaf of bread to keep them alive in their wretchedness, or gives them an entertainment to make them forget for an hour or two; but inspiration will cause them to rise out of their misery. If you want to help the poor, demonstrate to them that they can become rich; prove it by getting rich yourself.

The only way in which poverty will ever be banished from this world is by getting a large and constantly increasing number of people to practice the teachings of this book.

People must be taught to become rich by creation, not by competition.

Every man who becomes rich by competition throws down behind him the ladder by which he rises, and keeps others down; but every man who gets rich by creation opens a way for thousands to follow him, and inspires them to do so.

You are not showing hardness of heart or an unfeeling disposition when you refuse to pity poverty, see poverty, read about poverty, or think or talk about it, or to listen to those who do talk about it. Use your will power to keep your mind OFF the subject of poverty, and to keep it fixed with faith and purpose ON the vision of what you want.

Chapter Ten

FURTHER USE OF WILL

YOU cannot retain a true and clear vision of wealth if you are constantly turning your attention to opposing pictures, whether they be external or imaginary.

Do not tell of your past troubles of a financial nature, if you have had them, do not think of them at all. Do no tell of the poverty of your parents, or the hardships of your early life; to do any of these things is to mentally class yourself with the poor for the time being, and it will certainly check the movement of things in your direction.

"Let the dead bury their dead," as Jesus said. *let go of the past*

Put poverty and all things that pertain to poverty completely behind you.

You have accepted a certain theory of the universe as being correct, and are resting all your hopes of happiness on its being correct; and what can you gain by giving heed to conflicting theories?

Do not read religious books which tell you that the world is soon coming to an end; and do not read the writing of muck-rakers and pessimistic philosophers who tell you that it is going to the devil.

The world is not going to the devil; it is going to God.

It is wonderful Becoming.

True, there may be a good many things in existing conditions which are disagreeable; but what is the use of studying them when they are certainly passing away, and when the study of them only tends to check their passing and keep them with us? Why give time and attention to things which are being removed by evolutionary growth, when you can hasten their removal only by promoting the evolutionary growth as far as your part of it goes?

No matter how horrible in seeming may be the conditions in certain countries, sections, or places, you waste your time and destroy your own chances by considering them.

You should interest yourself in the world's becoming rich.

Think of the riches the world is coming into, instead of the poverty it is growing out of; and bear in mind that the only way in which you can assist the world in growing rich is by growing rich yourself through the creative method—not the competitive one.

Give your attention wholly to riches; ignore poverty.

Whenever you think or speak of those who are poor, think and speak of them as those who are becoming rich; as those who are to be congratulated rather than pitied. Then they and others will catch the inspiration, and begin to search for the way out.

Because I say that you are to give your whole time and mind and thought to riches, it does not follow that you are to be sordid or mean.

To become really rich is the noblest aim you can have in life, for it includes everything else.

On the competitive plane, the struggle to get rich is a Godless scramble for power over other men; but when we come into the creative mind, all this is changed.

All that is possible in the way of greatness and soul unfoldment, of service and lofty endeavor, comes by way of getting rich; all is made possible by the use of things.

If you lack for physical health, you will find that the attainment of it is conditional on your getting rich.

Only those who are emancipated from financial worry, and who have the means to live a care-free existence and follow hygienic practices, can have and retain health.

Moral and spiritual greatness is possible only to those who are above the competitive battle for existence; and only those who are becoming rich on the plane of creative thought are free from the degrading influences of competition. If your heart is set on domestic happiness, remember that love flourishes best where there is refinement, a high level of thought, and freedom from corrupting influences; and these are to be found only where riches are attained by the exercise of creative thought, without strife or rivalry.

You can aim at nothing so great or noble, I repeat, as to become rich; and you must fix your attention upon your mental picture of riches, to the exclusion of all that may tend to dim or obscure the vision.

You must learn to see the underlying TRUTH in all things; you must see beneath all seemingly wrong conditions the Great One Life ever moving forward toward fuller expression and more complete happiness.

It is the truth that there is no such thing as poverty; that there is only wealth.

Some people remain in poverty because they are ignorant of the fact that there is wealth for them; and these can best be taught by showing them the way to affluence in your own person and practice.

Others are poor because, while they feel that there is a way out, they are too intellectually indolent to put forth the

Money is a tool of advancement of life

mental effort necessary to find that way and by travel it; and for these the very best thing you can do is to arouse their desire by showing them the happiness that comes from being rightly rich.

Others still are poor because, while they have some notion of science, they have become so swamped and lost in the maze of metaphysical and occult theories that they do not know which road to take. They try a mixture of many systems and fail in all. For these, again, the very best thing, to do is to show the right way in your own person and practice; an ounce of doing things is worth a pound of theorizing.

The very best thing you can do for the whole world is to make the most of yourself.

You can serve God and man in no more effective way than by getting rich; that is, if you get rich by the creative method and not by the competitive one.

Another thing. We assert that this book gives in detail the principles of the science of getting rich; and if that is true, you do not need to read any other book upon the subject. This may sound narrow and egotistical, but consider: there is no more scientific method of computation in mathematics than by addition, subtraction, multiplication, and division; no other method is possible. There can be but one shortest distance between two points. There is only one way to think scientifically, and that is to think in the way that leads by the most direct and simple route to the goal. No man has yet formulated a briefer or less complex "system" than the one set forth herein; it has been stripped of all non-essentials. When you commence on this, lay all others aside; put them out of your mind altogether.

Read this book every day; keep it with you; commit it to memory, and do not think about other "systems" and theories. If you do, you will begin to have doubts, and to be uncertain and wavering in your thought; and then you will begin to make failures.

After you have made good and become rich, you may study other systems as much as you please; but until you are quite sure that you have gained what you want, do not read anything on this line but this book.

And read only the most optimistic comments on the world's news; those in harmony with your picture.

Also, postpone your investigations into the occult. Do not dabble in theosophy, Spiritualism, or kindred studies. It is very likely that the dead still live, and are near; but if they are, let them alone; mind your own business.

Wherever the spirits of the dead may be, they have their own work to do, and their own problems to solve; and we have no right to interfere with them. We cannot help them, and it is very doubtful whether they can help us, or whether we have any right to trespass upon their time if they can. Let the dead and the hereafter alone, and solve your own problem; get rich. If you begin to mix with the occult, you will start mental cross-currents which will surely bring your hopes to shipwreck. Now, this and the preceding chapters have brought us to the following statement of basic facts:—

There is a thinking stuff from which all things are made, and which, in its original state, permeates, penetrates, and fills the interspaces of the universe.

A thought, in this substance, Produces the thing that is imaged by the thought.

Man can form things in his thought, and, by impressing his thought upon formless substance, can cause the thing he thinks about to be created.

In order to do this, man must pass from the competitive to the creative mind; he must form a clear mental picture of the things he wants, and hold this picture in his thoughts with the fixed PURPOSE to get what he wants, and the unwavering FAITH that he does get what he wants, closing his mind against all that may tend to shake his purpose, dim his vision, or quench his faith.

And in addition to all this, we shall now see that he must live and act in a Certain Way.

Chapter Eleven

ACTING IN THE CERTAIN WAY

THOUGHT is the creative power, or the impelling force which causes the creative power to act; thinking in a Certain Way will bring riches to you, but you must not rely upon thought alone, paying no attention to personal action. That is the rock upon which many otherwise scientific metaphysical thinkers meet shipwreck—the failure to connect thought with personal action.

We have not yet reached the stage of development, even supposing such a stage to be possible, in which man can create directly from Formless Substance without nature's processes or the work of human hands; man must not only think, but his personal action must supplement his thought.

By thought you can cause the gold in the hearts of the mountains to be impelled toward you; but it will not mine itself, refine itself, coin itself into double eagles, and come rolling along the roads seeking its way into your pocket.

Under the impelling power of the Supreme Spirit, men's affairs will be so ordered that some one will be led to mine the gold for you; other men's business transactions will be so directed that the gold will be brought toward you, and you must so arrange your own business affairs that you may be able to receive it when it comes to you. Your thought makes all things, animate and inanimate, work to bring you what you want; but your personal activity must be such that you can rightly receive what you want when it reaches you. You are not to take it as charity, nor to steal it; you must give every man more in use value than he gives you in cash value.

The scientific use of thought consists in forming a clear and distinct mental image of what you want; in holding fast to the purpose to get what you want; and in realizing with grateful faith that you do get what you want.

Do not try to 'project' your thought in any mysterious or occult way, with the idea of having it go out and do things for you; that is wasted effort, and will weaken your power to think with sanity.

The action of thought in getting rich is fully explained in the preceding chapters; your faith and purpose positively impress your vision upon Formless Substance, which has THE SAME DESIRE FOR MORE LIFE THAT YOU HAVE; and this vision, received from you, sets all the creative forces at work IN AND THROUGH THEIR REGULAR CHANNELS OF ACTION, but directed toward you.

It is not your part to guide or supervise the creative process; all you have to do with that is to retain your vision, stick to your purpose, and maintain your faith and gratitude.

But you must act in a Certain Way, so that you can appropriate what is yours when it comes to you; so that you can meet the things you have in your picture, and put them in their proper places as they arrive.

You can really see the truth of this. When things reach you, they will be in the hands of other men, who will ask an equivalent for them.

And you can only get what is yours by giving the other man what is his.

Your pocketbook is not going to be transformed into a Fortunata's purse, which shall be always full of money without effort on your part.

This is the crucial point in the science of getting rich; right here, where thought and personal action must be combined. There are very many people who, consciously or unconsciously, set the creative forces in action by the strength and persistence of their desires, but who remain poor because they do not provide for the reception of the thing they want when it comes.

By thought, the thing you want is brought to you; by action you receive it.

Whatever your action is to be, it is evident that you must act NOW. You cannot act in the past, and it is essential to the clearness of your mental vision that you dismiss the past from

What do we want?

your mind. You cannot act in the future, for the future is not here yet. And you cannot tell how you will want to act in any future contingency until that contingency has arrived.

Because you are not in the right business, or the right environment now, do not think that you must postpone action until you get into the right business or environment. And do not spend time in the present taking thought as to the best course in possible future emergencies; have faith in your ability to meet any emergency when it arrives.

If you act in the present with your mind on the future, your present action will be with a divided mind, and will not be effective.

Put your whole mind into present action.

Do not give your creative impulse to Original Substance, and then sit down and wait for results; if you do, you will never get them. Act now. There is never any time but now, and there never will be any time but now. If you are ever to begin to make ready for the reception of what you want, you must begin now.

And your action, whatever it is, must most likely be in your present business or employment, and must be upon the persons and things in your present environment.

You cannot act where you are not; you cannot act where you have been, and you cannot act where you are going to be; you can act only where you are.

Do not bother as to whether yesterday's work was well done or ill done; do today's work well.

Do not try to do tomorrow's work now; there will be plenty of time to do that when you get to it.

Do not try, by occult or mystical means, to act on people or things that are out of your reach.

Do not wait for a change of environment, before you act; get a change of environment by action.

You can so act upon the environment in which you are now, as to cause yourself to be transferred to a better environment.

Hold with faith and purpose the vision of yourself in the better environment, but act upon your present environment with all your heart, and with all your strength, and with all your mind.

Do not spend any time in day dreaming or castle building; hold to the one vision of what you want, and act NOW.

Do not cast about seeking some new thing to do, or some strange, unusual, or remarkable action to perform as a first step toward getting rich. It is probable that your actions, at least for some time to come, will be those you have been performing for some time past; but you are to begin now to perform these actions in the Certain Way, which will surely make you rich.

Are my actions moving me towards my dream?

If you are engaged in some business, and feel that it is not the right one for you, do not wait until you get into the right business before you begin to act.

Do not feel discouraged, or sit down and lament because you are misplaced. No man was ever so misplaced but that he could not find the right place, and no man ever became so involved in the wrong business but that he could get into the right business.

Hold the vision of yourself in the right business, with the purpose to get into it, and the faith that you will get into it, and are getting into it; but ACT in your present business. Use your present business as the means of getting a better one, and use your present environment as the means of getting into a better one. Your vision of the right business, if held with faith and purpose, will cause the Supreme to move the right business toward you; and your action, if performed in the Certain Way, will cause you to move toward the business.

If you are an employee, or wage earner, and feel that you must change places in order to get what you want, do not 'project" your thought into space and rely upon it to get you another job. It will probably fail to do so.

Hold the vision of yourself in the job you want, while you ACT with faith and purpose on the job you have, and you will certainly get the job you want.

Your vision and faith will set the creative force in motion to bring it toward you, and your action will cause the forces in your own environment to move you toward the place you want. In closing this chapter, we will add another statement to our syllabus:—

There is a thinking stuff from which all things are made, and which, in its original state, permeates, penetrates, and fills the interspaces of the universe.

A thought, in this substance, Produces the thing that is imaged by the thought.

Man can form things in his thought, and, by impressing his thought upon formless substance, can cause the thing he thinks about to be created.

In order to do this, man must pass from the competitive to the creative mind; he must form a clear mental picture of the things he wants, and hold this picture in his thoughts with the fixed PURPOSE to get what he wants, and the unwavering FAITH that he does get what he wants, closing his mind to all that may tend to shake his purpose, dim his vision, or quench his faith.

That he may receive what he wants when it comes, man must act NOW upon the people and things in his present environment.

Chapter Twelve

EFFICIENT ACTION

YOU must use your thought as directed in previous chapters, and begin to do what you can do where you are; and you must do ALL that you can do where you are.

You can advance only be being larger than your present place; and no man is larger than his present place who leaves undone any of the work pertaining to that place.

The world is advanced only by those who more than fill their present places.

If no man quite filled his present place, you can see that there must be a going backward in everything. Those who do not quite fill their present places are dead weight upon society, government, commerce, and industry; they must be carried along by others at a great expense. The progress of the world is retarded only by those who do not fill the places they are holding; they belong to a former age and a lower stage or plane of life, and their tendency is toward degeneration. No society could advance if every man was smaller than his place; social evolution is guided by the law of physical and mental evolution. In the animal world, evolution is caused by excess of life.

When an organism has more life than can be expressed in the functions of its own plane, it develops the organs of a higher plane, and a new species is originated.

There never would have been new species had there not been organisms which more than filled their places. The law is exactly the same for you; your getting rich depends upon your applying this principle to your own affairs.

Every day is either a successful day or a day of failure; and it is the successful days which get you what you want. If everyday is a failure, you can never get rich; while if every day is a success, you cannot fail to get rich.

If there is something that may be done today, and you do not do it, you have failed in so far as that thing is concerned; and the consequences may be more disastrous than you imagine.

You cannot foresee the results of even the most trivial act; you do not know the workings of all the forces that have been set moving in your behalf. Much may be depending on your doing some simple act; it may be the very thing which is to open the door of opportunity to very great possibilities. You can never know all the combinations which Supreme Intelligence is making for you in the world of things and of things and of human affairs; your neglect or failure to do some small thing may cause a long delay in getting what you want.

Do, every day, ALL that can be done that day.

There is, however, a limitation or qualification of the above that you must take into account.

You are not to overwork, nor to rush blindly into your business in the effort to do the greatest possible number of things in the shortest possible time.

You are not to try to do tomorrow's work today, nor to do a week's work in a day.

It is really not he number of things you do, but the EFFICIENCY of each separate action that counts.

Every act is, in itself, either a success or a failure.

Every act is, in itself, either effective or inefficient.

Every inefficient act is a failure, and if you spend your life in doing inefficient acts, your whole life will be a failure.

The more things you do, the worse for you, if all your acts are inefficient ones.

On the other hand, every efficient act is a success in itself, and if every act of your life is an efficient one, your whole life MUST be a success.

Acts that produce results

The cause of failure is doing too many things in an inefficient manner, and not doing enough things in an efficient manner.

You will see that it is a self-evident proposition that if you do not do any inefficient acts, and if you do a sufficient number of efficient acts, you will become rich. If, now, it is possible for you to make each act an efficient one, you see again that the getting of riches is reduced to an exact science, like mathematics.

The matter turns, then, on the questions whether you can make each separate act a success in itself. And this you can certainly do.

You can make each act a success, because ALL Power is working with you; and ALL Power cannot fail.

Power is at your service; and to make each act efficient you have only to put power into it.

Every action is either strong or weak; and when every one is strong, you are acting in the Certain Way which will make you rich.

Every act can be made strong and efficient by holding your vision while you are doing it, and putting the whole power of your FAITH and PURPOSE into it.

It is at this point that the people fail who separate mental power from personal action. They use the power of mind in one place and at one time, and they act in another pace and at another time. So their acts are not successful in themselves; too many of them are inefficient. But if ALL Power goes into every act, no matter how commonplace, every act will be a success in itself; and as in the nature of things every success opens the way to other successes, your progress toward what you want, and the progress of what you want toward you, will become increasingly rapid.

Remember that successful action is cumulative in its results. Since the desire for more life is inherent in all things, when a man begins to move toward larger life more things attach themselves to him, and the influence of his desire is multiplied.

Do, every day, all that you can do that day, and do each act in an efficient manner.

In saying that you must hold your vision while you are doing each act, however trivial or commonplace, I do not mean to say that it is necessary at all times to see the vision distinctly to its smallest details. It should be the work of your leisure hours to use your imagination on the details of your vision, and to contemplate them until they are firmly fixed upon memory. If you wish speedy results, spend practically all your spare time in this practice.

By continuous contemplation you will get the picture of what you want, even to the smallest details, so firmly fixed upon your mind, and so completely transferred to the mind of Formless Substance, that in your working hours you need only to mentally refer to the picture to stimulate your faith and purpose, and cause your best effort to be put forth. Contemplate your picture in your leisure hours until your consciousness is so full of it that you can grasp it instantly. You will become so enthused with its bright promises that the mere thought of it will call forth the strongest energies of your whole being.

Let us again repeat our syllabus, and by slightly changing the closing statements bring it to the point we have now reached.

There is a thinking stuff from which all things are made, and which, in its original state, permeates, penetrates, and fills the interspaces of the universe.

A thought, in this substance, Produces the thing that is imaged by the thought.

Man can form things in his thought, and, by impressing his thought upon formless substance, can cause the thing he thinks about to be created.

In order to do this, man must pass from the competitive to the creative mind; he must form a clear mental picture of the things he wants, and do, with faith and purpose, all that can be done each day, doing each separate thing in an efficient manner.

Chapter Thirteen

GETTING INTO THE RIGHT BUSINESS

SUCCESS, in any particular business, depends for one thing upon your possessing in a well-developed state the faculties required in that business.

Without good musical faculty no one can succeed as a teacher of music; without well-developed mechanical faculties no one can achieve great success in any of the mechanical trades; without tact and the commercial faculties no one can succeed in mercantile pursuits. But to possess in a well-developed state the faculties required in your particular vocation does not insure getting rich. There are musicians who have remarkable talent, and who yet remain poor; there are blacksmiths, carpenters, and so on who have excellent mechanical ability, but who do not get rich; and there are merchants with good faculties for dealing with men who nevertheless fail.

The different faculties are tools; it is essential to have good tools, but it is also essential that the tools should be used in the Right Way. One man can take a sharp saw, a square, a good plane, and so on, and build a handsome article of furniture; another man can take the same tools and set to work to duplicate the article, but his production will be a botch. He does not know how to use good tools in a successful way.

The various faculties of your mind are the tools with which you must do the work which is to make you rich; it will be easier for you to succeed if you get into a business for which you are well equipped with mental tools.

Generally speaking, you will do best in that business which will use your strongest faculties; the one for which you are naturally "best fitted." But there are limitations to this statement, also. No man should regard his vocation as being irrevocably fixed by the tendencies with which he was born.

You can get rich in ANY business, for if you have not the right talent for you can develop that talent; it merely means that you will have to make your tools as you go along, instead of confining yourself to the use of those with which you were born. It will be EASIER for you to succeed in a vocation for which you already have the talents in a well-developed state; but you CAN succeed in any vocation, for you can develop any rudimentary talent, and there is no talent of which you have not at least the rudiment.

You will get rich most easily in point of effort, if you do that for which you are best fitted; but you will get rich most satisfactorily if you do that which you WANT to do.

Doing what you want to do is life; and there is no real satisfaction in living if we are compelled to be forever doing something which we do not like to do, and can never do what we want to do. And it is certain that you can do what you want to do; the **desire** to do it is proof that you have within you the power which **can** do it.

Desire is a manifestation of power.

The desire to play music is the power which can play music seeking expression and development; the desire to invent mechanical devices is the mechanical talent seeking expression and development.

Where there is no power, either developed or undeveloped, to do a thing, there is never any desire to do that thing; and where there is strong desire to do a thing, it is certain proof that the power to do it is strong, and only requires to be developed and applied in the Right Way.

All things else being equal, it is best to select the business for which you have the best developed talent; but if you have a strong desire to engage in any particular line of work, you should select that work as the ultimate end at which you aim.

You can do what you want to do, and it is your right and privilege to follow the business or avocation which will be most congenial and pleasant.

You are not obliged to do what you do not like to do, and should not do it except as a means to bring you to the doing of the thing you want to do.

If there are past mistakes whose consequences have placed you in an undesirable business or environment, you may be obliged for some time to do what you do not like to do; but you can make the doing of it pleasant by knowing that it is making it possible for you to come to the doing of what you want to do.

If you feel that you are not in the right vocation, do not act too hastily in trying to get into another one. The best way, generally, to change business or environment is by growth.

Do not be afraid to make a sudden and radical change if the opportunity is presented, and you feel after careful consideration that it is the right opportunity; but never take sudden or radical action when you are in doubt as to the wisdom of doing so.

There is never any hurry on the creative plane; and there is no lack of opportunity.

When you get out of the competitive mind you will understand that you never need to act hastily. No one else is going to beat you to the thing you want to do; there is enough for all. If one space is taken, another and a better one will be opened for you a little farther on; there is plenty of time. When you are in doubt, wait. Fall back on the contemplation of your vision, and increase your faith and purpose; and by all means, in times of doubt and indecision, cultivate gratitude.

A day or two spent in contemplating the vision of what you want, and in earnest thanksgiving that you are getting it, will bring your mind into such close relationship with the Supreme that you will make no mistake when you do act.

There is a mind which knows all there is to know; and you can come into close unity with this mind by faith and the purpose to advance in life, if you have deep gratitude.

Mistakes come from acting hastily, or from acting in fear or doubt, or in forgetfulness of the Right Motive, which is more life to all, and less to none.

As you go on in the Certain Way, opportunities will come to you in increasing number; and you will need to be very steady in your faith and purpose, and to keep in close touch with the All Mind by reverent gratitude.

Do all that you can do in a perfect manner every day, but do it without haste, worry, or fear. Go as fast as you can, but never hurry.

Remember that in the moment you begin to hurry you cease to be a creator and become a competitor; you drop back upon the old plane again.

Whenever you find yourself hurrying, call a halt; fix your attention on the mental image of the thing you want, and begin to give thanks that you are getting it. The exercise of GRATITUDE will never fail to strengthen your faith and renew your purpose.

Chapter Fourteen

THE IMPRESSION OF INCREASE

WHETHER you change your vocation or not, your actions for the present must be those pertaining to the business in which you are now engaged.

You can get into the business you want by making constructive use of the business you are already established in; by doing your daily work in a Certain Way.

And in so far as your business consists in dealing with other men, whether personally or by letter, the key-thought of all your efforts must be to convey to their minds the impression of increase.

Increase is what all men and all women are seeking; it is the urge of the Formless Intelligence within them, seeking fuller expression.

The desire for increase is inherent in all nature; it is the fundamental impulse of the universe. All human activities are based on the desire for increase; people are seeking more food, more clothes, better shelter, more luxury, more beauty, more knowledge, more pleasure—increase in something, more life.

Every living thing is under this necessity for continuous advancement; where increase of life ceases, dissolution and death set in at once.

Man instinctively knows this, and hence he is forever seeking more. This law of perpetual increase is set forth by Jesus in the parable of the talents; only those who gain more retain any; from him who hath not shall be taken away even that which he hath.

The normal desire for increased wealth is not an evil or a reprehensible thing; it is simply the desire for more abundant life; it is aspiration.

And because it is the deepest instinct of their natures, all men and women are attracted to him who can give them more of the means of life.

In following the Certain Way as described in the foregoing pages, you are getting continuous increase for yourself, and you are giving it to all with whom you deal.

You are a creative center, from which increase is given off to all.

Be sure of this, and convey assurance of the fact to every man, woman, and child with whom you come in contact. No matter how small the transaction, even if it be only the selling of a stick of candy to a little child, put into it the thought of increase, and make sure that the customer is impressed with the thought.

Convey the impression of advancement with everything you do, so that all people shall receive the impression that you are an Advancing Man, and that you advance all who deal with you. Even to the people whom you meet in a social way, without any thought of business, and to whom you do not try to sell anything, give the thought of increase.

You can convey this impression by holding the unshakable faith that you, yourself, are in the Way of Increase; and by letting this faith inspire, fill, and permeate every action.

Do everything that you do in the firm conviction that you are an advancing personality, and that you are giving advancement to everybody.

Feel that you are getting rich, and that in so doing you are making others rich, and conferring benefits on all.

Do not boast or brag of your success, or talk about it unnecessarily; true faith is never boastful.

Wherever you find a boastful person, you find one who is secretly doubtful and afraid. Simply feel the faith, and let it work out in every transaction; let every act and tone and look express the quiet assurance that you are getting rich; that you are already rich. Words will not be necessary to communicate this feeling to others; they will feel the sense of increase when in your presence, and will be attracted to you again.

You must so impress others that they will feel that in associating with you they will get increase for themselves. See that you give them a use value greater than the cash value you are taking from them.

Take an honest pride in doing this, and let everybody know it; and you will have no lack of customers. People will go where they are given increase; and the Supreme, which desires increase in all, and which knows all, will move toward you men and women who have never heard of you. Your business will increase rapidly, and you will be surprised at the unexpected benefits which will come to you. You will be able from day to day to make larger combinations, secure greater advantages, and to go on into a more congenial vocation if you desire to do so.

But doing thing all this, you must never lose sight of your vision of what you want, or your faith and purpose to get what you want.

Let me here give you another word of caution in regard to motives.

Beware of the insidious temptation to seek for power over other men.

Nothing is so pleasant to the unformed or partially developed mind as the exercise of power or dominion over others. *The desire to rule for selfish gratification has been the curse of the world.* For countless ages kings and lords have drenched the earth with blood in their battles to extend their dominions; this not to seek more life for all, but to get more power for themselves.

Today, the main motive in the business and industrial world is the same; men Marshal their armies of dollars, and lay waste the lives and hearts of millions in the same mad scramble for power over others. Commercial kings, like political kings, are inspired by the lust for power.

Jesus saw in this desire for mastery the moving impulse of that evil world He sought to overthrow. Read the twenty-third chapter of Matthew, and see how He pictures the lust of the Pharisees to be called "Master," to sit in the high places, to domineer over others, and to lay burdens on the backs of the less fortunate; and note how He compares this lust for dominion with the brotherly seeking for the Common Good to which He calls His disciples.

Look out for the temptation to seek for authority, to become a "master," to be considered as one who is above the common herd, to impress others by lavish display, and so on.

The mind that seeks for mastery over others is the competitive mind; and the competitive mind is not the creative one. In order to master your environment and your destiny, it is not at all necessary that you should rule over your fellow men and indeed, when you fall into the world's struggle for the high places, you begin to be conquered by fate and environment, and your getting rich becomes a matter of chance and speculation.

Beware of the competitive mind!! No better statement of the principle of creative action can be formulated than the favorite declaration of the late "Golden Rule" Jones of Toledo: "What I want for myself, I want for everybody."

Chapter Fifteen

THE ADVANCING MAN

WHAT I have said in the last chapter applies as well to the professional man and the wage-earner as to the man who is engaged in mercantile business.

No matter whether you are a physician, a teacher, or a clergyman, if you can give increase of life to others and make them sensible of the fact, they will be attracted to you, and you will get rich. The physician who holds the vision of himself as a great and successful healer, and who works toward the complete realization of that vision with faith and purpose, as described in former chapters, will come into such close touch with the Source of Life that he will be phenomenally successful; patients will come to him in throngs.

No one has a greater opportunity to carry into effect the teaching of this book than the practitioner of medicine; it does not matter to which of the various schools he may belong, for the principle of healing is common to all of them, and may be reached by all alike. The Advancing Man in medicine, who holds to a clear mental image of himself as successful, and who obeys the laws of faith, purpose, and gratitude, will cure every curable case he undertakes, no matter what remedies he may use.

In the field of religion, the world cries out for the clergyman who can teach his hearers the true science of abundant life. He who masters the details of the science of getting rich, together with the allied sciences of being well, of being great, and of winning love, and who teaches these details from the pulpit, will never lack for a congregation. This is the gospel that the world needs; it will give increase of life, and men will hear it gladly, and will give liberal support to the man who brings it to them.

What is now needed is a demonstration of the science of life from the pulpit. We want preachers who can not only tell us how, but who in their own persons will show us how. We need the preacher who will himself be rich, healthy, great, and beloved, to teach us how to attain to these things; and when he comes he will find a numerous and loyal following.

The same is true of the teacher who can inspire the children with the faith and purpose of the advancing life. He will never be "out of a job." And any teacher who has this faith and purpose can give it to his pupils; he cannot help giving it to them if it is part of his own life and practice.

What is true of the teacher, preacher, and physician is true of the lawyer, dentist, real estate man, insurance agent—of everybody.

The combined mental and personal action I have described is infallible; it cannot fail. Every man and woman who follows these instructions steadily, perseveringly, and to the letter, will get rich. The law of the Increase of Life is as mathematically certain in its operation as the law of gravitation; getting rich is an exact science.

The wage-earner will find this as true of his case as of any of the others mentioned. Do not feel that you have no chance to get rich because you are working where there is no visible opportunity for advancement, where wages are small and the cost of living high. Form your clear mental vision of what you want, and begin to act with faith and purpose.

Do all the work you can do, every day, and do each piece of work in a perfectly successful manner; put the power of success, and the purpose to get rich, into everything that you do.

But do not do this merely with the idea of currying favor with your employer, in the hope that he, or those above you, will see your good work and advance you; it is not likely that they will do so.

The man who is merely a "good" workman, filling his place to the very best of his ability, and satisfied with that, is valuable to his employer; and it is not to the employer's interest to promote him; he is worth more where he is.

To secure advancement, something more is necessary than to be too large for your place.

The man who is certain to advance is the one who is too big for his place, and who has a clear concept of what he wants to be; who knows that he can become what he wants to be and who is determined to BE what he wants to be.

Do not try to more than fill your present place with a view to pleasing your employer; do it with the idea of advancing yourself. Hold the faith and purpose of increase during work hours, after work hours, and before work hours. Hold it in such a way that every person who comes in contact with you, whether foreman, fellow workman, or social acquaintance, will feel the power of purpose radiating from you; so that every one will get the sense of advancement and increase from you. Men will be attracted to you, and if there is no possibility for advancement in your present job, you will very soon see an opportunity to take another job.

There is a Power which never fails to present opportunity to the Advancing Man who is moving in obedience to law.

God cannot help helping you, if you act in a Certain Way; He must do so in order to help Himself.

There is nothing in your circumstances or in the industrial situation that can keep you down. If you cannot get rich working for the steel trust, you can get rich on a ten-acre farm; and if you begin to move in the Certain Way, you will certainly escape from the "clutches" of the steel trust and get on to the farm or wherever else you wish to be.

If a few thousands of its employees would enter upon the Certain Way, the steel trust would soon be in a bad plight; it would have to give its workingmen more opportunity, or go out of business. Nobody has to work for a trust; the trusts can keep men in so called hopeless conditions only so long as there are men who are too ignorant to know of the science of getting rich, or too intellectually slothful to practice it.

Begin this way of thinking and acting, and your faith and purpose will make you quick to see any opportunity to better your condition.

Such opportunities will speedily come, for the Supreme, working in All, and working for you, will bring them before you.

Do not wait for an opportunity to be all that you want to be; when an opportunity to be more than you are now is presented and you feel impelled toward it, take it. It will be the first step toward a greater opportunity.

There is no such thing possible in this universe as a lack of opportunities for the man who is living the advancing life.

It is inherent in the constitution of the cosmos that all things shall be for him and work together for his good; and he must certainly get rich if he acts and thinks in the Certain Way. So let wage-earning men and women study this book with great care, and enter with confidence upon the course of action it prescribes; it will not fail.

Chapter Sixteen

SOME CAUTION, AND CONCLUDING OBSERVATIONS

MANY people will scoff at the idea that there is an exact science of getting rich; holding the impression that the supply of wealth is limited, they will insist that social and governmental institutions must be changed before even any considerable number of people can acquire a competence.

But this is not true.

It is true that existing governments keep the masses in poverty, but this is because the masses do not think and act in the Certain Way.

If the masses begin to move forward as suggested in this book, neither governments nor industrial systems can check them; all systems must be modified to accommodate the forward movement.

If the people have the Advancing Mind, have the Faith that they can become rich, and move forward with the fixed purpose to become rich, nothing can possibly keep them in poverty.

Individuals may enter upon the Certain Way at any time, and under any government, and make themselves rich; and when any considerable number of individuals do so under any government, they will cause the system to be so modified as to open the way for others.

The more men who get rich on the competitive plane, the worse for others; the more who get rich on the creative plane, the better for others.

The economic salvation of the masses can only be accomplished by getting a large number of people to practice the scientific method set down in this book, and become rich. These will show others the way, and inspire them with a desire for real life, with the faith that it can be attained, and with the purpose to attain it.

For the present, however, it is enough to know that neither the government under which you live nor the capitalistic or competitive system of industry can keep you from getting rich. When you enter upon the creative plane of thought you will rise above all these things and become a citizen of another kingdom.

But remember that your thought must be held upon the creative plane; you are never for an instant to be betrayed into regarding the supply as limited, or into acting on the moral level of competition.

Whenever you do fall into old ways of thought, correct yourself instantly; for when you are in the competitive mind, you have lost the cooperation of the Mind of the Whole.

Do not spend any time in planning as to how you will meet possible emergencies in the future, except as the necessary policies may affect your actions today. You are concerned with doing today's work in a perfectly successful manner, and not with emergencies which may arise tomorrow; you can attend to them as they come.

Do not concern yourself with questions as to how you shall surmount obstacles which may loom upon your business horizon, unless you can see plainly that your course must be altered today in order to avoid them.

No matter how tremendous an obstruction may appear at a distance, you will find that if you go on in the Certain Way it will disappear as you approach it, or that a way over, though, or around it will appear.

No possible combination of circumstances can defeat a man or woman who is proceeding to get rich along strictly scientific lines. No man or woman who obeys the law can fail to get rich, any more than one can multiply two by two and fail to get four.

Give no anxious thought to possible disasters, obstacles, panics, or unfavorable combinations of circumstances; it is time enough to meet such things when they present themselves before you in the immediate present, and you will find that every difficulty carries with it the wherewithal for its overcoming.

Guard your speech. Never speak of yourself, your affairs, or of anything else in a discouraged or discouraging way.

Never admit the possibility of failure, or speak in a way that infers failure as a possibility.

Never speak of the times as being hard, or of business conditions as being doubtful. Times may be hard and business doubtful for those who are on the competitive plane, but they can never be so for you; you can create what you want, and you are above fear.

When others are having hard times and poor business, you will find your greatest opportunities.

Train yourself to think of and to look upon the world as a something which is Becoming, which is growing; and to regard seeming evil as being only that which is undeveloped. Always speak in terms of advancement; to do otherwise is to deny your faith, and to deny your faith is to lose it.

Never allow yourself to feel disappointed. You may expect to have a certain thing at a certain time, and not get it at that time; and this will appear to you like failure.

But if you hold to your faith you will find that the failure is only apparent.

Go on in the certain way, and if you do not receive that thing, you will receive something so much better that you will see that the seeming failure was really a great success.

A student of this science had set his mind on making a certain business combination which seemed to him at the time to be very desirable, and he worked for some, weeks to bring it about. When the crucial time came, the thing failed in a perfectly inexplicable way; it was as if some unseen influence had been working secretly against him. He was not disappointed; on the contrary, he thanked God that his desire had been overruled, and went steadily on with a grateful mind. In a few weeks an opportunity so much better came his way that he would not have made the first deal on any account; and he saw that a Mind which knew more than he knew had prevented him from losing the greater good by entangling himself with the lesser.

That is the way every seeming failure will work out for you, if you keep your faith, hold to your purpose, have gratitude, and do, every day, all that can be done that day, doing each separate act in a successful manner.

When you make a failure, it is because you have not asked for enough; keep on, and a larger thing then you were seeking will certainly come to you. Remember this.

You will not fail because you lack the necessary talent to do what you wish to do. If you go on as I have directed, you will develop all the talent that is necessary to the doing of your work.

It is not within the scope of this book to deal with the science of cultivating talent; but it is as certain and simple as the process of getting rich.

However, do not hesitate or waver for fear that when you come to any certain place you will fail for lack of ability; keep right on, and when you come to that place, the ability will be furnished to you. The same source of Ability which enabled the untaught Lincoln to do the greatest work in government ever accomplished by a single man is open to you; you may draw upon all the mind there is for wisdom to use in meeting the responsibilities which are laid upon you. Go on in full faith.

Study this book. Make it your constant companion until you have mastered all the ideas contained in it. While you are getting firmly established in this faith, you will do well to give up most recreations and pleasure; and to stay away from places where ideas conflicting with these are advanced in lectures or sermons. Do not read pessimistic or conflicting literature, or get into arguments upon the matter. Do very little reading, outside of the writers mentioned in the Preface. Spend most of your leisure time in contemplating your vision, and in cultivating gratitude, and in reading this book. It contains all you need to know of the science of getting rich; and you will find all the essentials summed up in the following chapter.

Chapter Seventeen

SUMMARY OF
THE SCIENCE OF GETTING RICH

THERE is a thinking stuff from which all things are made, and which, in its original state, permeates, penetrates, and fills the interspaces of the universe.

A thought in this substance produces the thing that is imaged by the thought.

Man can form things in his thought, and by impressing his thought upon formless substance can cause the thing he thinks about to be created.

In order to do this, man must pass from the competitive to the creative mind; else he cannot be in harmony with the Formless Intelligence, which is always creative and never competitive in spirit.

Man may come into full harmony with the Formless Substance by entertaining a lively and sincere gratitude for the blessings it bestows upon him. Gratitude unifies the mind of man with the intelligence of Substance, so that man's thoughts are received by the Formless. Man can remain upon the creative plane only by uniting himself with the Formless

Intelligence through a deep and continuous feeling of gratitude .

Man must form a clear and definite mental image of the things he wishes to have, to do, or to become; and he must hold this mental image in his thoughts, while being deeply grateful to the Supreme that all his desires are granted to him. The man who wishes to get rich must spend his leisure hours in contemplating his Vision, and in earnest thanksgiving that the reality is being given to him. Too much stress cannot be laid on the importance of frequent contemplation of the mental image, coupled with unwavering faith and devout gratitude. This is the process by which the impression is given to the Formless, and the creative forces set in motion.

The creative energy works through the established channels of natural growth, and of the industrial and social order. All that is included in his mental image will surely be brought to the man who follows the instructions given above, and whose faith does not waver. What he wants will come to him through the ways of established trade and commerce.

In order to receive his own when it shall come to him, man must be active; and this activity can only consist in more than filling his present place. He must keep in mind the Purpose to get rich through the realization of his mental image. And he must do, every day, all that can be done that day, taking care to do each act in a successful manner. He must give to every man a use value in excess of the cash value he receives, so that each transaction makes for more life; and he must so hold the Advancing Thought that the impression of increase will be communicated to all with whom he comes in contact.

The men and women who practice the foregoing instructions will certainly get rich; and the riches they receive will be in exact proportion to the definiteness of their vision, the fixity of their purpose, the steadiness of their faith, and the depth of their gratitude

THE
PATH
OF
PROSPERITY

by
James allen

CONTENTS

Chapter One

THE LESSON OF EVIL

Unrest and pain and sorrow are the shadows of life. There is no heart in all the world that has not felt the sting of pain, no mind has not been tossed upon the dark waters of trouble, no eye that has not wept the hot blinding tears of unspeakable anguish.

There is no household where the Great Destroyers, disease and death, have not entered, severing heart from heart, and casting over all the dark pall of sorrow.

In the strong, and apparently indestructible meshes of evil all are more or less fast caught, and pain, unhappiness, and misfortune wait upon mankind.

With the object of escaping, or in some way mitigating this overshadowing gloom, men and women rush blindly into innumerable devices, pathways by which they fondly hope to enter into a happiness which will not pass away.

Such are the drunkard and the harlot, who revel in sensual excitements; such is the exclusive aesthete, who shuts himself out from the sorrows of the world, and surrounds himself with enervating luxuries; such is he who thirsts for wealth or fame, and subordinates all things to the achievement of that object; and such are they who seek consolation in the performance of religious rites.

And to all the happiness sought seems to come, and the soul, for a time, is lulled into a sweet security, and an intoxicating forgetfulness of the existence of evil; but the day of disease comes at last, or some great sorrow, temptation, or misfortune breaks suddenly in on the unfortified soul, and the fabric of its fancied happiness is torn to shreds.

So over the head of every personal joy hangs the Damocletian sword of pain, ready, at any moment, to fall and crush the soul of him who is unprotected by knowledge.

The child cries to be a man or woman; the man and woman sigh for the lost felicity of childhood. The poor man chafes under the chains of poverty by which he is bound, and the rich man often lives in fear of poverty, or scours the world in search of an elusive shadow he calls happiness.

Sometimes the soul feels that it has found a secure peace and happiness in adopting a certain religion, in embracing an intellectual philosophy, or in building up an intellectual or artistic ideal; but some overpowering temptation proves the religion to be inadequate or insufficient; the theoretical philosophy is found to be a useless prop; or in a moment, the idealistic statue upon which the devotee has for years been laboring, is shattered into fragments at his feet.

Is there, then, no way of escape from pain and sorrow? Are there no means by which bonds of evil may be broken? Is permanent happiness, secure prosperity, and abiding peace a foolish dream?

No, there is a way, and I speak it with gladness, by which evil can be slain for ever; there is a process by which disease, poverty, or any adverse condition or circumstance can be put on one side never to return; there is a method by which a permanent prosperity can be secured, free from all fear of the return of adversity, and there is a practice by which unbroken and unending peace and bliss can be partaken of and realized.

And the beginning of the way which leads to this glorious realization is the acquirement of a right understanding of the nature of evil.

It is not sufficient to deny or ignore evil; it must be understood. It is not enough to pray to God to remove the evil; you must find out why it is there, and what lesson it has for you.

It is of no avail to fret and fume and chafe at the chains which bind you; you must know why and how you are bound. Therefore, reader, you must get outside yourself, and must begin to examine and understand yourself.

You must cease to be a disobedient child in the school of experience and must begin to learn, with humility and patience, the lessons that are set for your edification and ultimate perfection; for evil, when rightly understood, is found to be, not an unlimited power or principle in the universe, but a passing phase of human experience, and it therefore becomes a teacher to those who are willing to learn.

Evil is not an abstract some thing outside yourself; it is an experience in your own heart, and by patiently examining and rectifying your heart you will be gradually led into the discovery of the origin and nature of evil, which will necessarily be followed by its complete eradication.

All evil is corrective and remedial, and is therefore not permanent. It is rooted in ignorance, ignorance of the true nature and relation of things, and so long as we remain in that state of ignorance, we remain subject to evil.

There is no evil in the universe which is not the result of ignorance, and which would not, if we were ready and willing to learn its lesson, lead us to higher wisdom, and then vanish away. But men remain in evil, and it does not pass away because men are not willing or prepared to learn the lesson which it came to teach them.

I knew a child who, every night when its mother took it to bed, cried to be allowed to play with the candle; and one night, when the mother was off guard for a moment, the child took hold of the candle; the inevitable result followed, and the child never wished to play with the candle again.

By its one foolish act it learned, and learned perfectly the lesson of obedience, and entered into the knowledge that fire burns.

And, this incident is a complete illustration of the nature, meaning, and ultimate result of all sin and evil.

As the child suffered through its own ignorance of the real nature of fire, so older children suffer through their ignorance of the real nature of the things which they weep for and strive after, and which harm them when they are secured; the only difference being that in the latter case the ignorance and evil are more deeply rooted and obscure.

Evil has always been symbolized by darkness, and Good by light, and hidden within the symbol is contained the perfect interpretation, the reality; for, just as light always floods the universe, and darkness is only a mere speck or shadow cast by a small body intercepting a few rays of the illimitable

light, so the Light of the Supreme Good is the positive and life-giving power which floods the universe, and evil the insignificant shadow cast by the self that intercepts and shuts off the illuminating rays which strive for entrance.

When night folds the world in its black impenetrable mantle, no matter how dense the darkness, it covers but the small space of half our little planet, while the whole universe is ablaze with living light, and every soul knows that it will awake in the light in the morning.

Know, then, that when the dark night of sorrow, pain, or misfortune settles down upon your soul, and you stumble along

with weary and uncertain steps, that you are merely intercepting your own personal desires between yourself and the boundless light of joy and bliss, and the dark shadow that covers you is cast by none and nothing but yourself.

And just as the darkness without is but a negative shadow, an unreality which comes from nowhere, goes to nowhere, and has no abiding dwelling place, so the darkness within is equally a negative shadow passing over the evolving and Light-born soul.

"But," I fancy I hear someone say, "why pass through the darkness of evil at all?" Because, by ignorance, you have chosen to do so, and because, by doing so, you may understand both good and evil, and may the more appreciate the light by having passed through the darkness.

As evil is the direct outcome of ignorance, so, when the lessons of evil are fully learned, ignorance passes away, and wisdom takes its place. But as a disobedient child refuses to learn its lessons at school, so it is possible to refuse to learn the lessons of experience, and thus to remain in continual darkness, and to suffer continually recurring punishments in the form of disease, disappointment, and sorrow.

He, therefore, who would shake himself free of the evil which encompasses him, must be willing and ready to learn, and must be prepared to undergo that disciplinary process without which no grain of wisdom or abiding happiness and peace can be secured.

A man may shut himself up in a dark room, and deny that the light exists, but it is everywhere without, and darkness exists only in his own little room.

So you may shut out the light of Truth, or you may begin to pull down the walls of prejudice, self-seeking and error which you have built around yourself, and so let in the glorious and omnipresent Light.

By earnest self-examination strive to realize, and not merely hold as a theory, that evil is a passing phase, a self-created shadow; that all your pains, sorrows and misfortunes have come to you by a process of undeviating and absolutely perfect law; have come to you because you deserve and require them, and that by first enduring, and then understanding them, you may be made stronger, wiser, nobler.

When you have fully entered into this realization, you will be in a position to mould your own circumstances, to transmute all evil into good and to weave, with a master hand, the fabric of your destiny.

What of the night, O Watchman! see'st thou yet
The glimmering dawn upon the mountain heights,
The golden Herald of the Light of lights,
Are his fair feet upon the hilltops set?

Cometh he yet to chase away the gloom,
And with it all the demons of the Night?
Strike yet his darting rays upon thy sight?
Hear'st thou his voice, the sound of error's doom?

The Morning cometh, lover of the Light;
Even now He gilds with gold the mountain's brow,
Dimly I see the path whereon even now
His shining feet are set toward the Night.

Darkness shall pass away, and all the things
That love the darkness, and that hate the Light
Shall disappear for ever with the Night:
Rejoice! for thus the speeding Herald sings.

Chapter TWO

THE WORLD A REFLEX
OF MENTAL STATES

WHAT you are, so is your world. Everything in the universe is resolved into your own inward experience. It matters little what is without, for it is all a reflection of your own state of consciousness.

It matters everything what you are within, for everything without will be mirrored and colored accordingly.

All that you positively know is contained in your own experience; all that you ever will know must pass through the gateway of experience, and so become part of yourself.

Your own thoughts, desires, and aspirations comprise your world, and, to you, all that there is in the universe of beauty and joy and bliss, or of ugliness and sorrow and pain, is contained within yourself.

By your own thoughts you make or mar your life, your world, your universe, As you build within by the power of thought, so will your outward life and circumstances shape themselves accordingly.

Whatsoever you harbor in the inmost chambers of your heart will, sooner or later by the inevitable law of reaction, shape itself in your outward life.

The soul that is impure, sordid and selfish, is gravitating with unerring precision toward misfortune and catastrophe; the soul that is pure, unselfish, and noble is gravitating with equal precision toward happiness and prosperity.

Every soul attracts its own, and nothing can possibly come to it that does not belong to it. To realize this is to recognize the universality of Divine Law.

The incidents of every human life, which both make and mar, are drawn to it by the quality and power of its own inner thought-life. Every soul is a complex combination of gathered experiences and thoughts, and the body is but an improvised vehicle for its manifestation.

What, therefore, your thoughts are, that is your real self; and the world around, both animate and inanimate, wears the aspect with which your thoughts clothe it. "All that we are is the result of what we have thought. It is founded on our thoughts; it is made up of our thoughts." Thus said Buddha, and it therefore follows that if a man is happy, it is because he dwells in happy thoughts; if miserable, because he dwells in despondent and debilitating thoughts,

Whether one be fearful or fearless, foolish or wise, troubled or serene, within that soul lies the cause of its own state or states, and never without. And now I seem to hear a chorus of voices exclaim, "But do you really mean to say that outward circumstances do not affect our minds?" I do not say that, but I say this, and know it to be an infallible truth, that circumstances can only affect you in so far as you allow them to do so.

You are swayed by circumstances because you have not a right understanding of the nature, use, and power of thought.

You believe (and upon this little word belief hang all our sorrows and joys) that outward things have the power to make or mar your life; by so doing you submit to those outward things, confess that you are their slave, and they your unconditional master; by so doing, you invest them with a power which they do not, of themselves, possess, and you succumb, in reality, not to the mere circumstances, but to the gloom or gladness, the fear or hope, the strength or weakness, which your thought-sphere has thrown around them.

I knew two men who, at an early age, lost the hard-earned savings of years. One was very deeply troubled, and gave way to chagrin, worry, and despondency.

The other, on reading in his morning paper that the bank in which his money was deposited had hopelessly failed, and that he had lost all, quietly and firmly remarked, "Well, it's gone, and trouble and worry won't bring it back, but hard work will."

He went to work with renewed vigor, and rapidly became prosperous, while the former man, continuing to mourn the loss of his money, and to grumble at his "bad luck," remained the sport and tool of adverse circumstances, in reality of his own weak and slavish thoughts.

The loss of money was a curse to the one because he clothed the event with dark and dreary thoughts; it was a blessing to the other, because he threw around it thoughts of strength, of hope, and renewed endeavor.

If circumstances had the power to bless or harm, they would bless and harm all men alike, but the fact that the same circumstances will be alike good and bad to different souls proves that the good or bad is not in the circumstance, but only in the mind of him that encounters it.

When you begin to realize this you will begin to control your thoughts, to regulate and discipline your mind, and to rebuild the inward temple of your soul, eliminating all useless and superfluous material, and incorporating into your being thoughts alone of joy and serenity, of strength and life, of compassion and love, of beauty and immortality; and as you do this you will become joyful and serene, strong and healthy, compassionate and loving, and beautiful with the beauty of immortality.

And as we clothe events with the drapery of our own thoughts, so likewise do we clothe the objects of the visible world around us, and where one sees harmony and beauty, another sees revolting ugliness.

An enthusiastic naturalist was one day roaming the country lanes in pursuit of his hobby, and during his rambles came upon a pool of brackish water near a farmyard.

As he proceeded to fill a small bottle with the water for the purpose of examination under the microscope, he dilated, with more enthusiasm than discretion, to an uncultivated son of the plough who stood close by, upon the hidden and innumerable wonders contained in the pool, and concluded by saying, "Yes, my friend, within this pool is contained a hundred, nay, a million universes, had we but the sense or the instrument by which we could apprehend them." And the unsophisticated one ponderously remarked, "I know the water be full o' tadpoles, but they be easy to catch."

Where the naturalist, his mind stored with the knowledge of natural facts, saw beauty, harmony, and hidden glory, the mind unenlightened upon those things saw only an offensive mud-puddle.

The wild flower which the casual wayfarer thoughtlessly tramples upon is, to the spiritual eye of the poet, an angelic messenger from the invisible.

To the many, the ocean is but a dreary expanse of water on which ships sail and are sometimes wrecked; to the soul of the musician it is a living thing, and he hears, in all its changing moods, divine harmonies.

Where the ordinary mind sees disaster and confusion, the mind of the philosopher sees the most perfect sequence of cause and effect, and where the materialist sees nothing but endless death, the mystic sees pulsating and eternal life.

And as we clothe both events and objects with our own thoughts, so likewise do we clothe the souls of others in the garments of our thoughts.

The suspicious believe everybody to be suspicious; the Liar feels secure in the thought that he is not so foolish as to believe that there is such a phenomenon as a strictly truthful person; the envious see envy in every soul; the miser thinks everybody is eager to get his money; he who has subordinated conscience in the making of his wealth, sleeps with a revolver under his pillow, wrapped in the delusion that the world is full of conscienceless people who are eager to rob him, and the abandoned sensualist looks upon the saint as a hypocrite.

On the other hand, those who dwell in loving thoughts, see that in all which calls forth their love and sympathy; the trusting and honest are not troubled by suspicions; the good-natured and charitable who rejoice at the good fortune of others, scarcely know what envy means; and he who has realized the Divine within himself recognizes it in all beings, even in the beasts.

And men and women are confirmed in their mental outlook because of the fact that, by the law of cause and effect, they attract to themselves that which they send forth, and so come in contact with people similar to themselves.

The old adage, "Birds of a feather flock together," has a deeper significance than is generally attached to it, for in the thought-world as in the world of matter, each clings to its kind.

> *Do you wish for kindness? Be kind.*
> *Do you ask for truth? Be true.*
> *What you give of yourself you find;*
> *Your world is a reflex of you.*

If you are one of those who are praying for, and looking forward to, a happier world beyond the grave, here is a message of gladness for you, you may enter into and realize that happy world now; it fills the whole universe, and it is within you, waiting for you to find, acknowledge, and possess. Said one who knew the inner laws of Being, "When men shall say lo here, or lo there, go not after them; the kingdom of God is within you."

What you have to do is to believe this, simply believe it with a mind unshadowed by doubt, and then meditate upon it till you understand it.

You will then begin to purify and to build your inner world, and as you proceed, passing from revelation to revelation, from realization to realization, you will discover the utter powerlessness of outward things beside the magic potency of a self-governed soul.

If thou would'st right the world,
And banish all its evils and its woes,
Make its wild places bloom,
And its drear deserts blossom as the rose,—
Then right thyself.

If thou would'st turn the world
From its long, lone captivity in sin,
Restore all broken hearts,
Slay grief, and let sweet consolation in,—
Turn thou thyself.

If thou would'st cure the world
Of its long sickness, end its grief and pain;
Bring in all-healing joy,
And give to the afflicted rest again,—
Then cure thyself.

If thou would'st wake the world
Out of its dream of death and dark'ning strife,
Bring it to Love and Peace,
And Light and brightness of immortal Life,—
Wake thou thyself.

Chapter Three

THE WAY OUT OF UNDESIRABLE CONDITIONS

HAVING seen and realized that evil is but a passing shadow thrown, by the intercepting self, across the transcendent Form of the Eternal Good, and that the world is a mirror in which each sees a reflection of himself, we now ascend, by firm and easy steps, to that plane of perception whereon is seen and realized the Vision of the Law.

With this realization comes the knowledge that everything is included in a ceaseless interaction of cause and effect, and that nothing can possibly be divorced from law.

From the most trivial thought, word, or act of man, up to the groupings of the celestial bodies, law reigns supreme. No arbitrary condition can, even for one moment, exist, for such a condition would be a denial and an annihilation of law.

Every condition of life is, therefore, bound up in an orderly and harmonious sequence, and the secret and cause of every condition is contained within itself, The law, "Whatsoever a man sows that shall he also reap," is inscribed in flaming letters upon the portal of Eternity, and none can deny it, none can cheat it, none can escape it.

He who puts his hand in the fire must suffer the burning until such time as it has worked itself out, and neither curses nor prayers can avail to alter it.

And precisely the same law governs the realm of mind. Hatred, anger, jealousy, envy, lust, covetousness, all these are fires which bum, and whoever even so much as touches them must suffer the torments of burning.

All these conditions of mind are rightly called "evil," for they are the efforts of the soul to subvert, in its ignorance, the law, an they, therefore, lead to chaos and confusion within, and are sooner or later actualized in the outward circumstances as disease, failure, and misfortune, coupled with grief, pain, and despair.

Whereas love, gentleness, good-will, purity, are cooling airs which breathe peace upon the soul that woes them, and, being in harmony with the Eternal Law, they become actualized in the form of health, peaceful surroundings, and undeviating success and good fortune.

A thorough understanding of this Great Law which permeates the universe leads to the acquirement of that state of mind known as obedience.

To know that justice, harmony, and love are supreme in the universe is likewise to know that all adverse and painful conditions are the result of our own disobedience to that Law.

Such knowledge leads to strength and power, and it is upon such knowledge alone that a true life and an enduring success and happiness can be built.

To be patient under all circumstances, and to accept all conditions as necessary factors in your training, is to rise superior to all painful conditions, and to overcome them with an overcoming which is sure, and which leaves no fear of their return, for by the power of obedience to law they are utterly slain.

Such an obedient one is working in harmony with the law, has in fact, identified himself with the law, and whatsoever he conquers he conquers for ever, whatsoever he builds can never be destroyed.

The cause of all power, as of all weakness, is within; the secret of all happiness as of all misery is likewise within.

There is no progress apart from unfoldment within, and no sure foothold of prosperity or peace except by orderly advancement in knowledge.

You say you are chained by circumstances; you cry out for better opportunities, for a wider scope, for improved physical conditions, and perhaps you inwardly curse the fate that binds you hand and foot.

It is for you that I write; it is to you that I speak. Listen, and let my words burn themselves into your heart, for that which I say to you is truth:

You may bring about that improved condition in your outward life which you desire, if you will unswervingly resolve to improve your inner life.

I know this pathway looks barren at its commencement (truth always does, it is only error and delusion which are at first inviting and fascinating,) but if you undertake to walk it; if you perseveringly discipline your mind, eradicating your weaknesses, and allowing your soul-forces and spiritual powers to unfold themselves, you will be astonished at the magical changes which will be brought about in your outward life.

As you proceed, golden opportunities will be strewn across your path, and the power and judgment to properly utilize them will spring up within you. Genial friends will come unbidden to you; sympathetic souls will be drawn to you as the needle is to the magnet; and books and all outward aids that you require will come to you unsought.

Perhaps the chains of poverty hang heavily upon you, and you are friendless and alone, and you long with an intense longing that your load may be lightened; but the load continues, and you seem to be enveloped in an ever-increasing darkness.

Perhaps you complain, you bewail your lot; you blame your birth, your parents, your employer, or the unjust Powers who have bestowed upon you so undeservedly poverty and hardship, and upon another affluence and ease.

Cease your complaining and fretting; none of these things which you blame are the cause of your poverty; the cause is within yourself, and where the cause is, there is the remedy.

The very fact that you are a complainer, shows that you deserve your lot; shows that you lack that faith which is the ground of all effort and progress.

There is no room for a complainer in a universe of law, and worry is soul-suicide. By your very attitude of mind you are strengthening the chains which bind you, and are drawing about you the darkness by which you are enveloped, Alter your outlook upon life, and your outward life will alter.

Build yourself up in the faith and knowledge, and make yourself worthy of better surroundings and wider opportunities. Be sure, first of all, that you are making the best of what you have.

Do not delude yourself into supposing that you can step into greater advantages whilst overlooking smaller ones, for if you could, the advantage would be impermanent and you would quickly fall back again in order to learn the lesson which you had neglected.

As the child at school must master one standard before passing onto the next, so, before you can have that greater good which you so desire, must you faithfully employ that which you already possess.

The parable of the talents is a beautiful story illustrative of this truth, for does it not plainly show that if we misuse, neglect, or degrade that which we possess, be it ever so mean and insignificant, even that little will be taken from us, for, by our conduct we show that we are unworthy of it.

Perhaps you are living in a small cottage, and are surrounded by unhealthy and vicious influences.

You desire a larger and more sanitary residence. Then you must fit yourself for such a residence by first of all making your cottage as far as possible a little paradise.

Keep it spotlessly clean. Make it look as pretty and sweet as your limited means will allow. Cook your plain food with all care, and arrange your humble table as tastefully as you possibly can.

If you cannot afford a carpet, let your rooms be carpeted with smiles and welcomes, fastened down with the nails of kind words driven in with the hammer of patience. Such a carpet will not fade in the sun, and constant use will never wear it away.

By so ennobling your present surroundings you will rise above them, and above the need of them, and at the right time you will pass on into the better house and surroundings which have all along been waiting for you, and which you have fitted yourself to occupy.

Perhaps you desire more time for thought and effort, and feel that your hours of labor are too hard and long. Then see to it that you are utilizing to the fullest possible extent what little spare time you have.

It is useless to desire more time, if you are already wasting what little you have; for you would only grow more indolent and indifferent.

Even poverty and lack of time and leisure are not the evils that you imagine they are, and if they hinder you in your progress, it is because you have clothed them in your own weaknesses, and the evil that you see in them is really in yourself.

Endeavor to fully and completely realize that in so far as you shape and mould your mind, you are the maker of your destiny, and as, by the transmuting power of self-discipline you realize this more and more, you will come to see that these so-called evils may be converted into blessings.

You will then utilize your poverty for the cultivation of patience, hope and courage; and your lack of time in the gaining of promptness of action and decision of mind, by seizing the precious moments as they present themselves for your acceptance.

As in the rankest soil the most beautiful flowers are grown, so in the dark soil of poverty the choicest flowers of humanity have developed and bloomed.

Where there are difficulties to cope with, and unsatisfactory conditions to overcome, there virtue most flourishes and manifests its glory.

It may be that you are in the employ of a tyrannous master or mistress, and you feel that you are harshly treated. Look upon this also as necessary to your training. Return your employer's unkindness with gentleness and forgiveness.

Practice unceasingly patience and self-control. Turn the disadvantage to account by utilizing it for the gaining of mental and spiritual strength, and by your silent example and influence you will thus be teaching your employer, will be helping him to grow ashamed of his conduct, and will, at the same time, be lifting yourself up to that height of spiritual attainment by which you will be enabled to step into new and more congenial surroundings at the time when they are presented to you.

Do not complain that you are a slave, but lift yourself up, by noble conduct, above the plane of slavery. Before complaining that you are a slave to another, be sure that you are not a slave to self.

Look within; look searchingly, and have no mercy upon yourself. You will find there, perchance, slavish thoughts, slavish desires, and in your daily life and conduct slavish habits.

Conquer these; cease to be a slave to self, and no man will have the power to enslave you. As you overcome self, you will overcome all adverse conditions, and every difficulty will fall before you.

Do not complain that you are oppressed by the rich. Are you sure that if you gained riches you would not be an oppressor yourself?

Remember that there is the Eternal Law which is absolutely just, and that he who oppresses today must himself be oppressed tomorrow; and from this there is no way of escape.

And perhaps you, yesterday (in some former existence) were rich and an oppressor, and that you are now merely paying off the debt which you owe to the Great Law. Practice, therefore, fortitude and faith.

Dwell constantly in mind upon the Eternal justice, the Eternal Good. Endeavor to lift yourself above the personal and the transitory into the impersonal and permanent.

Shake off the delusion that you are being injured or oppressed by another, and try to realize, by a profounder comprehension of your inner life, and the laws which govern that life, that you are only really injured by what is within you. There is no practice more degrading, debasing, and soul-destroying than that of self-pity.

Cast it out from you. While such a canker is feeding upon your heart you can never expect to grow into a fuller life.

Cease from the condemnation of others, and begin to condemn yourself. Condone none of your acts, desires or thoughts that will not bear comparison with spotless purity, or endure the light of sinless good.

By so doing you will be building your house upon the rock of the Eternal, and all that is required for your happiness and well-being will come to you in its own time.

There is positively no way of permanently rising above poverty, or any undesirable condition, except by eradicating those selfish and negative conditions within, of which these are the reflection, and by virtue of which they continue.

The way to true riches is to enrich the soul by the acquisition of virtue. Outside of real heart-virtue there is neither prosperity nor power, but only the appearances of these. I am aware that men make money who have acquired no measure of virtue, and have little desire to do so; but such money does not constitute true riches, and its possession is transitory and feverish.

Here is David's testimony:— "For I was envious at the foolish when I saw the prosperity of the wicked... Their eyes stand out with fatness; they have more than heart could wish... Verily I have cleansed my heart in vain, and washed my hands in innocence... When I thought to know this it was too painful for me; until I went into the sanctuary of God, then understood I their end."

The prosperity of the wicked was a great trial to David until he went into the sanctuary of God, and then he knew their end.

You likewise may go into that sanctuary. It is within you. It is that state of consciousness which remains when all that is sordid, and personal, and impermanent is risen above, and universal and eternal principles are realized.

That is the God state of consciousness; it is the sanctuary of the Most High. When by long strife and self-discipline, you have succeeded in entering the door of that holy Temple, you will perceive, with unobstructed vision, the end and fruit of all human thought and endeavor, both good and evil.

You will then no longer relax your faith when you see the immoral man accumulating outward riches, for you will know, that he must come again to poverty and degradation.

The rich man who is barren of virtue is, in reality, poor, and as surely, as the waters of the river are drifting to the ocean, so surely is he, in the midst of all his riches, drifting towards poverty and misfortune; and though he die rich, yet must he return to reap the bitter fruit of all of his immorality.

And though he become rich many times, yet as many times must he be thrown back into poverty, until, by long experience and suffering he conquers the poverty within.

But the man who is outwardly poor, yet rich in virtue, is truly rich, and, in the midst of all his poverty he is surely traveling towards prosperity; and abounding joy and bliss await his coming. If you would become truly and permanently prosperous, you must first become virtuous.

It is therefore unwise to aim directly at prosperity, to make it the one object of life, to reach out greedily for it, To do this is to ultimately defeat yourself.

But rather aim at self-perfection, make useful and unselfish service the object of your life, and ever reach out hands of faith towards the supreme and unalterable Good.

You say you desire wealth, not for your own sake, but in order to do good with it, and to bless others. If this is your real motive in desiring wealth, then wealth will come to you; for you are strong and unselfish indeed if, in the midst of riches, you are willing to look upon yourself as steward and not as owner.

But examine well your motive, for in the majority of instances where money is desired for the admitted object of blessing others, the real underlying motive is a love of popularity, and a desire to pose as a philanthropist or reformer.

If you are not doing good with what little you have, depend upon it the more money you got the more selfish you would become, and all the good you appeared to do with your money, if you attempted to do any, would be so much insinuating self-laudation.

If your real desire is to do good, there is no need to wait for money before you do it; you can do it now, this very moment, and just where you are. If you are really so unselfish as you believe yourself to be, you will show it by sacrificing yourself for others now.

No matter how poor you are, there is room for self-sacrifice, for did not the widow put her all into the treasury?

The heart that truly desires to do good does not wait for money before doing it, but comes to the altar of sacrifice and, leaving there the unworthy elements of self, goes out and breathes upon neighbor and stranger, friend and enemy alike the breath of blessedness.

As the effect is related to the cause, so is prosperity and power related to the inward good and poverty and weakness to the inward evil.

Money does not constitute true wealth, nor position, nor power, and to rely upon it alone is to stand upon a slippery place.

Your true wealth is your stock of virtue, and your true power the uses to which you put it. Rectify your heart, and you will rectify your life. Lust, hatred, anger, vanity, pride, covetousness, self-indulgence, self-seeking, obstinacy,— all these are poverty and weakness; whereas love, purity, gentleness, meekness, compassion, generosity, self-forgetfulness, and self-renunciation,—all these are wealth and power.

As the elements of poverty and weakness are overcome, an irresistible and all-conquering power is evolved from within, and he who succeeds in establishing himself in the highest virtue, brings the whole world to his feet.

But the rich, as well as the poor, have their undesirable conditions, and are frequently farther removed from happiness than the poor. And here we see how happiness depends, not upon outward aids or possessions, but upon the inward life.

Perhaps you are an employer, and you have endless trouble with those whom you employ, and when you do get good and faithful servants they quickly leave you. As a result you are beginning to lose, or have completely lost, your faith in human nature.

You try to remedy matters by giving better wages, and by allowing certain liberties, yet matters remain unaltered. Let me advise you.

The secret of all your trouble is not in your servants, it is in yourself; and if you look within, with a humble and sincere desire to discover and eradicate your error, you will, sooner or later, find the origin of all your unhappiness.

It may be some selfish desire, or lurking suspicion, or unkind attitude of mind which sends out its poison upon those about you, and reacts upon yourself, even though you may not show it in your manner or speech.

Think of your servants with kindness, consider of them that extremity of service which you yourself would not care to perform were you in their place.

Rare and beautiful is that humility of soul by which a servant entirely forgets himself in his master's good; but far rarer, and beautiful with a divine beauty, is that nobility of soul by which a man, forgetting his own happiness, seeks the happiness of those who are under his authority, and who depend upon him for their bodily sustenance.

And such a man's happiness is increased tenfold, nor does he need to complain of those whom he employs. Said a well known and extensive employer of labor, who never needs to dismiss an employee: "I have always had the happiest relations with my workpeople. If you ask me how it is to be accounted for, I can only say that it has been my aim from the first to do to them as I would wish to be done by." Herein lies the secret by which all desirable conditions are secured, and all that are undesirable are overcome.

Do you say that you are lonely and unloved, and have "not a friend in the world"? Then, I pray you, for the sake of your own happiness, blame nobody but yourself.

Be friendly towards others, and friends will soon flock round you. Make yourself pure and lovable, and you will be loved by all.

Whatever conditions are rendering your life burdensome, you may pass out of and beyond them by developing and utilizing within you the transforming power of self-purification and self-conquest.

Be it the poverty which galls (and remember that the poverty upon which I have been dilating is that poverty which is a source of misery, and not that voluntary poverty which is the glory of emancipated souls), or the riches which burden, or the many misfortunes, griefs, and annoyances which form the dark background in the web of life, you may overcome them by overcoming the selfish elements within which give them life.

It matters not that by the unfailing Law, there are past thoughts and acts to work out and to atone for, as, by the same law, we are setting in motion, during every moment of our life, fresh thoughts and acts, and we have the power to make them good or ill.

Nor does it follow that if a man (reaping what he has sown) must lose money or forfeit position, that he must also lose his fortitude or forfeit his uprightness, and it is in these that his wealth and power and happiness are to be found.

He who clings to self is his own enemy and is surrounded by enemies.

He who relinquishes self is his own savior, and is surrounded by friends like a protecting belt. Before the divine radiance of a pure heart all darkness vanishes and all clouds melt away, and he who has conquered self has conquered the universe.

Come, then, out of your poverty; come out of your pain; come out of your troubles, and sighings, and complainings, and heartaches, and loneliness by coming out of yourself.

Let the old tattered garment of your petty selfishness fall from you, and put on the new garment of universal Love. You will then realize the inward heaven, and it will be reflected in all your outward life.

He who sets his foot firmly upon the path of self-conquest, who walks, aided by the staff of Faith, the highway of self-sacrifice, will assuredly achieve the highest prosperity, and will reap abounding and enduring joy and bliss.

To them that seek the highest good
All things subserve the wisest ends;
Nought comes as ill, and wisdom lends
Wings to all shapes of evil brood.

The dark'ning sorrow veils a Star
That waits to shine with gladsome light;
Hell waits on heaven; and after night
Comes golden glory from afar.

Defeats are steps by which we climb
With purer aim to nobler ends;
Loss leads to gain, and joy attends
True footsteps up the hills of time.

Pain leads to paths of holy bliss,
To thoughts and words and deeds divine-,
And clouds that gloom and rays that shine,
Along life's upward highway kiss.

Misfortune does but cloud the way
Whose end and summit in the sky
Of bright success, sunkiss'd and high,
Awaits our seeking and our stay.

The heavy pall of doubts and fears
That clouds the Valley of our hopes,
The shades with which the spirit copes,
The bitter harvesting of tears,

The heartaches, miseries, and griefs,
The bruisings born of broken ties,
All these are steps by which we rise
To living ways of sound beliefs.

Love, pitying, watchful, runs to meet
The Pilgrim from the Land of Fate;
All glory and all good await
The coming of obedient feet.

Chapter Four

THE SILENT POWER OF THOUGHT: CONTROLLING AND DIRECTING ONE'S FORCES

THE most powerful forces in the universe are the silent forces; and in accordance with the intensity of its power does a force become beneficent when rightly directed, and destructive when wrongly employed.

This is a common knowledge in regard to the mechanical forces, such as steam, electricity, etc., but few have yet learned to apply this knowledge to the realm of mind, where the thought-forces (most powerful of all) are continually being generated and sent forth as currents of salvation or destruction.

At this stage of his evolution, man has entered into the possession of these forces, and the whole trend of his present advancement is their complete subjugation. All the wisdom possible to man on this material earth is to be found only in complete self-mastery, and the command, "Love your enemies," resolves itself into an exhortation to enter here and now, into the possession of that sublime wisdom by taking hold of, mastering and transmuting, those mind forces to which man is now slavishly subject, and by which he is helplessly borne, like a straw on the stream, upon the currents of selfishness.

The Hebrew prophets, with their perfect knowledge of the Supreme Law, always related outward events to inward thought, and associated national disaster or success with the thoughts and desires that dominated the nation at the time.

The knowledge of the causal power of thought is the basis of all their prophecies, as it is the basis of all real wisdom and power. National events are simply the working out of the psychic forces of the nation.

Wars, plagues, and famines are the meeting and clashing of wrongly-directed thought-forces, the culminating points at which destruction steps in as the agent of the Law.

It is foolish to ascribe war to the influence of one man, or to one body of men. It is the crowning horror of national selfishness. It is the silent and conquering thought-forces which bring all things into manifestation.

The universe grew out of thought. Matter in its last analysis is found to be merely objectivized thought. All men's accomplishments were first wrought out in thought, and then objectivized.

The author, the inventor, the architect, first builds up his work in thought, and having perfected it in all its parts as a complete and harmonious whole upon the thought-plane. he then commences to materialize it, to bring it down to the material or sense-plane.

When the thought-forces are directed in harmony with the over-ruling Law, they are up-building and preservative, but when subverted they become disintegrating and self-destructive.

To adjust all your thoughts to a perfect and unswerving faith in the omnipotence and supremacy of Good, is to co-operate with that Good, and to realize within yourself the solution and destruction of all evil. Believe and ye shall live.

And here we have the true meaning of salvation; salvation from the darkness and negation of evil, by entering into, and realizing the living light of the Eternal Good.

Where there is fear, worry, anxiety, doubt, trouble, chagrin, or disappointment, there is ignorance and lack of faith.

All these conditions of mind are the direct outcome of selfishness, and are based upon an inherent belief in the power and supremacy of evil; they therefore constitute practical atheism; and to live in, and become subject to, these negative and soul-destroying conditions of mind is the only real atheism.

It is salvation from such conditions that the race needs, and let no man boast of salvation whilst he is their helpless and obedient slave.

To fear or to worry is as sinful as to curse, for how can one fear or worry if he intrinsically believes in the Eternal justice, the Omnipotent Good, the Boundless Love? To fear, to worry, to doubt, is to deny, to dis-believe.

It is from such states of mind that all weakness and failure proceed, for they represent the annulling and disintegrating of the positive thought-forces which would otherwise speed to their object with power, and bring about their own beneficent results.

To overcome these negative conditions is to enter into a life of power, is to cease to be a slave, and to become a master, and there is only one way by which they can be overcome, and that is by steady and persistent growth in inward knowledge.

To mentally deny evil is not sufficient; it must, by daily practice, be risen above and understood. To mentally affirm the good is inadequate; it must, by unswerving endeavor, be entered into and comprehended.

The intelligent practice of self-control, quickly leads to a knowledge of one's interior thought-forces, and, later on, to the acquisition of that power by which they are rightly employed and directed.

In the measure that you master self, that you control your mental forces instead of being controlled by them, in just such measure will you master affairs and outward circumstances.

Show me a man under whose touch everything crumbles away, and who cannot retain success even when it is placed in his hands, and I will show you a man who dwells continually in those conditions of mind which are the very negation of power.

To be for ever wallowing in the bogs of doubt, to be drawn continually into the quicksands of fear, or blown ceaselessly about by the winds of anxiety, is to be a slave, and to live the life of a slave, even though success and influence be for ever knocking at your door seeking for admittance.

Such a man, being without faith and without self-government, is incapable of the right government of his affairs, and is a slave to circumstances; in reality a slave to himself. Such are taught by affliction, and ultimately pass from weakness to strength by the stress of bitter experience. Faith and purpose constitute the motive-power of life.

There is nothing that a strong faith and an unflinching purpose may not accomplish. By the daily exercise of silent faith, the thought-forces are gathered together, and by the daily strengthening of silent purpose, those forces are directed toward the object of accomplishment.

Whatever your position in life may be, before you can hope to enter into any measure of success, usefulness, and power, you must learn how to focus your thought-forces by cultivating calmness and repose. It may be that you are a business man, and you are suddenly confronted with some overwhelming difficulty or probable disaster. You grow fearful and anxious, and are at your wit's end.

To persist in such a state of mind would be fatal, for when anxiety steps in, correct judgment passes out. Now if you will take advantage of a quiet hour or two in the early morning or at night, and go away to some solitary spot, or to some room in your house where you know you will be absolutely free from intrusion, and, having seated yourself in an easy attitude, you forcibly direct your mind right away from the object of anxiety by dwelling upon something in your life that is pleasing and blissgiving, a calm, reposeful strength will gradually steal into your mind, and your anxiety will pass away.

Upon the instant that you find your mind reverting to the lower plane of worry bring it back again, and re-establish it on the plane of peace and strength.

When this is fully accomplished, you may then concentrate your whole mind upon the solution of your difficulty, and what was intricate and insurmountable to you in your hour of anxiety will be made plain and easy, and you will see, with that clear vision and perfect judgment which belong only to a calm and untroubled mind, the right course to pursue and the proper end to be brought about.

It may be that you will have to try day after day before you will be able to perfectly calm your mind, but if you persevere you will certainly accomplish it. And the course which is presented to you in that hour of calmness must be carried out.

Doubtless when you are again involved in the business of the day, and worries again creep in and begin to dominate you, you will begin to think that the course is a wrong or foolish one, but do not heed such suggestions.

Be guided absolutely and entirely by the vision of calmness, and not by the shadows of anxiety. The hour of calmness is the hour of illumination and correct judgment.

By such a course of mental discipline the scattered thought-forces are re-united, and directed, like the rays of the search-light, upon the problem at issue, with the result that it gives way before them.

There is no difficulty, however great, but will yield before a calm and powerful concentration of thought, and no legitimate object but may be speedily actualized by the intelligent use and direction of one's soul-forces.

Not until you have gone deeply and searchingly into your inner nature, and have overcome many enemies that lurk there, can you have any approximate conception of the subtle power of thought, of its inseparable relation to outward and material things, or of its magical potency, when rightly poised and directed, in readjusting and transforming the life-conditions.

Every thought you think is a force sent out, and in accordance with its nature and intensity will it go out to seek a lodgment in minds receptive to it, and will react upon yourself for good or evil. There is ceaseless reciprocity between mind and mind, and a continual interchange of thought-forces.

Selfish and disturbing thoughts are so many malignant and destructive forces, messengers of evil, sent out to stimulate and augment the evil in other minds, which in turn send them back upon you with added power.

While thoughts that are calm, pure, and unselfish are so many angelic messengers sent out into the world with health, healing, and blessedness upon their wings, counteracting the evil forces; pouring the oil of joy upon the troubled waters of anxiety and sorrow, and restoring to broken hearts their heritage of immortality.

Think good thoughts, and they will quickly become actualized in your outward life in the form of good conditions. Control your soul-forces, and you will be able to shape your outward life as you will.

The difference between a savior and a sinner is this, that the one has a perfect control of all the forces within him; the other is dominated and controlled by them.

There is absolutely no other way to true power and abiding peace, but by self-control, self-government, self-purification. To be at the mercy of your disposition is to be impotent, unhappy, and of little real use in the world.

The conquest of your petty likes and dislikes, your capricious loves and hates, your fits of anger, suspicion, jealousy, and all the changing moods to which you are more or less helplessly subject, this is the task you have before you if you would weave into the web of life the golden threads of happiness and prosperity.

In so far as you are enslaved by the changing moods within you, will you need to depend upon others and upon outward aids as you walk through life.

If you would walk firmly and securely, and would accomplish any achievement, you must learn to rise above and control all such disturbing and retarding vibrations.

You must daily practice the habit of putting your mind at rest, "going into the silence," as it is commonly called. This is a method of replacing a troubled thought with one of peace, a thought of weakness with one of strength.

Until you succeed in doing this you cannot hope to direct your mental forces upon the problems and pursuits of life with any appreciable measure of success. It is a process of diverting one's scattered forces into one powerful channel.

Just as a useless marsh may be converted into a field of golden corn or a fruitful garden by draining and directing the scattered and harmful streams into one well-cut channel, so, he who acquires calmness, and subdues and directs the thought-currents within himself, saves his soul, and fructifies his heart and life.

As you succeed in gaining mastery over your impulses and thoughts you will begin to feel, growing up within you, a new and silent power, and a settled feeling of composure and strength will remain with you.

Your latent powers will begin to unfold themselves, and whereas formerly your efforts were weak and ineffectual, you will now be able to work with that calm confidence which commands success.

And along with this new power and strength, there will be awakened within you that interior Illumination known as "intuition," and you will walk no longer in darkness and speculation, but in light and certainty.

With the development of this soul-vision, judgment and mental penetration will be incalculably increased, and there will evolve within you that prophetic vision by the aid of which you will be able to sense coming events, and to forecast, with remarkable accuracy, the result of your efforts.

And in just the measure that you alter from within will your outlook upon life alter; and as you alter your mental attitude towards others they will alter in their attitude and conduct toward you.

As you rise above the lower, debilitating, and destructive thought-forces, you will come in contact with the positive, strengthening, and up-building currents generated by strong, pure, and noble minds, your happiness will be immeasurably intensified, and you will begin to realize the joy, strength, and power, which are born only of self-mastery.

And this joy, strength, and power will be continually radiating from you, and without any effort on your part, nay, though you are utterly unconscious of it, strong people will be drawn toward you, influence will be put into your hands, and in accordance with your altered thought-world will outward events shape themselves.

"A man's foes are they of his own household," and he who would be useful, strong, and happy, must cease to be a passive receptacle for the negative, beggarly, and impure streams of thought; and as a wise householder commands his servants and invites his guests, so must he learn to command his desires, and to say, with authority, what thoughts he shall admit into the mansion of his soul.

Even a very partial success in self-mastery adds greatly to one's power, and he who succeeds in perfecting this divine accomplishment, enters into possession of undreamed-of wisdom and inward strength and peace, and realizes that all the forces of the universe aid and protect his footsteps who is master of his soul.

Would you scale the highest heaven,
Would you pierce the lowest hell,
Live in dreams of constant beauty,
Or in basest thinkings dwell.

For your thoughts are heaven above you,
And your thoughts are hell below,
Bliss is not, except in thinking,
Torment nought but thought can know.

Worlds would vanish but for thinking;
Glory is not but in dreams;
And the Drama of the ages
From the Thought Eternal streams.

Dignity and shame and sorrow,
Pain and anguish, love and hate
Are but maskings of the mighty
Pulsing Thought that governs Fate.

As the colors of the rainbow
Makes the one uncolored beam,
So the universal changes
Make the One Eternal Dream.

And the Dream is all within you,
And the Dreamer waiteth long
For the Morning to awake him
To the living thought and strong.

That shall make the ideal real,
Make to vanish dreams of hell
In the highest, holiest heaven
Where the pure and perfect dwell.

Evil is the thought that thinks it;
Good, the thought that makes it so
Light and darkness, sin and pureness
Likewise out of thinking grow.

Dwell in thought upon the Grandest,
And the Grandest you shall see;
Fix your mind upon the Highest,
And the Highest you shall be.

Chapter Five

THE SECRET OF HEALTH, SUCCESS AND POWER

WE all remember with what intense delight, as children, we listened to the never-tiring fairy-tale. How eagerly we followed the fluctuating fortunes of the good boy or girl, ever protected, in the hour of crisis, from the evil machinations of the scheming witch, the cruel giant, or the wicked king.

And our little hearts never faltered for the fate of the hero or heroine, nor did we doubt their ultimate triumph over all their enemies, for we knew that the fairies were infallible, and that they would never desert those who had consecrated themselves to the good and the true.

And what unspeakable joy pulsated within us when the Fairy-Queen, bringing all her magic to bear at the critical moment, scattered all the darkness and trouble, and granted them the complete satisfaction of all their hopes, and they were "happy ever after."

With the accumulating years, and an ever-increasing intimacy with the so-called " realities" of life, our beautiful fairy-world became obliterated, and its wonderful inhabitants were relegated, in the archives of memory, to the shadowy and unreal.

And we thought we were wise and strong in thus leaving for ever the land of childish dreams, but as we re-become little children in the wondrous world of wisdom, we shall return again to the inspiring dreams of childhood and find that they are, after all, realities.

The fairy-folk, so small and nearly always invisible, yet possessed of an all-conquering and magical power, who bestow upon the good, health, wealth, and happiness, along with all the gifts of nature in lavish profusion, start again into reality and become immortalized in the soul-realm of him who, by growth in wisdom, has entered into a knowledge of the power of thought, and the laws which govern the inner world of being.

To him the fairies live again as thought-people, thought-messengers, thought-powers working in harmony with the over-ruling Good. And they who, day by day, endeavor to harmonize their hearts with the heart of the Supreme Good, do in reality acquire true health, wealth, and happiness.

There is no protection to compare with goodness, and by "goodness" I do not mean a mere outward conformity to the rules of morality; I mean pure thought, noble aspiration, unselfish love, and freedom from vainglory.

To dwell continually in good thoughts, is to throw around oneself a psychic atmosphere of sweetness and power which leaves its impress upon all who come in contact with it.

As the rising sun puts to rout the helpless shadows, so are all the impotent forces of evil put to flight by the searching rays of positive thought which shine forth from a heart made strong in purity and faith.

Where there is sterling faith and uncompromising purity there is health, there is success, there is power. In such a one, disease, failure, and disaster can find no lodgment, for there is nothing on which they can feed.

Even physical conditions are largely determined by mental states, and to this truth the scientific world is rapidly being drawn.

The old, materialistic belief that a man is what his body makes him, is rapidly passing away, and is being replaced by the inspiring belief that man is superior to his body, and that his body is what he makes it by the power of thought.

Men everywhere are ceasing to believe that a man is despairing because he is dyspeptic, and are coming to understand that he is dyspeptic because he is despairing, and in the near future, the fact that all disease has its origin in the mind will become common knowledge.

There is no evil in the universe but has its root and origin in the mind, and sin, sickness, sorrow, and affliction do not, in reality, belong to the universal order, are not inherent in the nature of things, but are the direct outcome of our ignorance of the right relations of things.

According to tradition, there once lived, in India, a school of philosophers who led a life of such absolute purity and simplicity that they commonly reached the age of one hundred and fifty years, and to fall sick was looked upon by them as an unpardonable disgrace, for it was considered to indicate a violation of law.

The sooner we realize and acknowledge that sickness, far from being the arbitrary visitation of an offended God, or the test of an unwise Providence, is the result of our own error or sin, the sooner shall we enter upon the highway of health.

Disease comes to those who attract it, to those whose minds and bodies are receptive to it, and flees from those whose strong, pure, and positive thought-sphere generates healing and life-giving currents.

If you are given to anger, worry, jealousy, greed, or any other inharmonious state of mind, and expect perfect physical health, you are expecting the impossible, for you are continually sowing the seeds of disease in your mind.

Such conditions of mind are carefully shunned by the wise man, for he knows them to be far more dangerous than a bad drain or an infected house.

If you would be free from all physical aches and pains, and would enjoy perfect physical harmony, then put your mind in order, and harmonize your thoughts. Think joyful thoughts; think loving thoughts; let the elixir of goodwill course through your veins, and you will need no other medicine. Put away your jealousies, your suspicions, your worries, your hatreds, your selfish indulgences, and you will put away your dyspepsia, your biliousness, your nervousness and aching joints.

If you will persist in clinging to these debilitating and demoralizing habits of mind, then do not complain when your body is laid low with sickness. The following story illustrates the close relation that exists between habits of mind and bodily conditions.

A certain man was afflicted with a painful disease, and he tried one physician after another, but all to no purpose. He then visited towns which were famous for their curative waters, and after having bathed in them all, his disease was more painful than ever.

One night he dreamed that a Presence came to him and said, "Brother, hast thou tried all the means of cure?" and he replied, "I have tried all." "Nay," said the Presence, "Come with me, and I will show thee a healing bath which has escaped thy notice."

The afflicted man followed, and the Presence led him to a clear pool of water, and said, "Plunge thyself in this water and thou shalt surely recover," and thereupon vanished.

The man plunged into the water, and on coming out, lo! his disease had left him, and at the same moment he saw written above the pool the word "Renounce." Upon waking, the fall meaning of his dream flashed across his mind, and looking within he discovered that he had, all along, been a victim to a sinful indulgence, and he vowed that he would renounce it for ever.

He carried out his vow, and from that day his affliction began to leave him, and in a short time he was completely restored to health. Many people complain that they have broken down through over-work. In the majority of such cases the breakdown is more frequently the result of foolishly wasted energy.

If you would secure health you must learn to work without friction. To become anxious or excited, or to worry over needless details is to invite a breakdown.

Work, whether of brain or body, is beneficial and health-giving, and the man who can work with a steady and calm persistency, freed from all anxiety and worry, and with his mind utterly oblivious to all but the work he has in hand, will not only accomplish far more than the man who is always hurried and anxious, but he will retain his health, a boon which the other quickly forfeits.

True health and true success go together, for they are inseparably intertwined in the thought-realm. As mental harmony produces bodily health, so it also leads to a harmonious sequence in the actual working out of one's plans.

Order your thoughts and you will order your life. Pour the oil of tranquility upon the turbulent waters of the passions and prejudices, and the tempests of misfortune, howsoever they may threaten, will be powerless to wreck the barque of your soul, as it threads its way across the ocean of life.

And if that barque be piloted by a cheerful and never-failing faith its course will be doubly sure, and many perils will pass it by which would other-wise attack it.

By the power of faith every enduring work is accomplished. Faith in the Supreme; faith in the over-ruling Law; faith in your work, and in your power to accomplish that work,— here is the rock upon which you must build if you would achieve, if you would stand and not fall.

To follow, under all circumstances, the highest promptings within you; to be always true to the divine self; to rely upon the inward Light, the inward Voice, and to pursue your purpose with a fearless and restful heart, believing that the future will yield unto you the meed of every thought and effort; knowing that the laws of the universe can never fail, and that your own will come back to you with mathematical exactitude, this is faith and the living of faith.

By the power of such a faith the dark waters of uncertainty are divided, every mountain of difficulty crumbles away, and the believing soul passes on unharmed.

Strive, O reader! to acquire, above everything, the priceless possession of this dauntless faith, for it is the talisman of happiness, of success, of peace, of power, of all that makes life great and superior to suffering.

Build upon such a faith, and you build upon the Rock of the Eternal, and with the materials of the Eternal, and the structure that you erect will never be dissolved, for it will transcend all the accumulations of material luxuries and riches, the end of which is dust.

Whether you are hurled into the depths of sorrow or lifted upon the heights of joy, ever retain your hold upon this faith, ever return to it as your rock of refuge, and keep your feet firmly planted upon its immortal and immovable base.

Centered in such a faith, you will become possessed of such a spiritual strength as will shatter, like so many toys of glass, all the forces of evil that are hurled against you, and you will achieve a success such as the mere striver after worldly gain can never know or even dream of. "If ye have faith, and doubt not, ye shall not only do this, ... but if ye shall say unto this mountain, be thou removed and be thou cast into the sea, it shall be done."

There are those today, men and women tabernacled in flesh and blood, who have realized this faith, who live in it and by it day by day, and who, having put it to the uttermost test, have entered into the possession of its glory and peace.

Such have sent out the word of command, and the mountains of sorrow and disappointment, of mental weariness and physical pain have passed from them, and have been cast into the sea of oblivion.

If you will become possessed of this faith you will not need to trouble about your success or failure, and success will come.

You will not need to become anxious about results, but will work joyfully and peacefully, knowing that right thoughts and right efforts will inevitably bring about right results.

I know a lady who has entered into many blissful satisfactions, and recently a friend remarked to her, "Oh, how fortunate you are! You only have to wish for a thing, and it comes to you."

And it did, indeed, appear so on the surface; but in reality all the blessedness that has entered into this woman's life is the direct outcome of the inward state of blessedness which she has, throughout life, been cultivating and training toward perfection.

Mere wishing brings nothing but disappointment; it is living that tells.

The foolish wish and grumble; the wise, work and wait. And this woman had worked; worked without and within, but especially within upon heart and soul; and with the invisible hands of the spirit she had built up, with the precious stones of faith, hope, joy, devotion, and love, a fair temple of light, whose glorifying radiance was ever round about her.

It beamed in her eye; it shone through her countenance; it vibrated in her voice; and all who came into her presence felt its captivating spell.

And as with her, so with you. Your success, your failure, your influence, your whole life you carry about with you, for your dominant trends of thought are the determining factors in your destiny.

Send forth loving, stainless, and happy thoughts, and blessings will fall into your hands, and your table will be spread with the cloth of peace.

Send forth hateful, impure, and unhappy thoughts, and curses will rain down upon you, and fear and unrest will wait upon your pillow. You are the unconditional maker of your fate, be that fate what it may. Every moment you are sending forth from you the influences which will make or mar your life.

Let your heart grow large and loving and unselfish, and great and lasting will be your influence and success, even though you make little money.

Confine it within the narrow limits of self-interest, and even though you become a millionaire your influence and success, at the final reckoning will be found to be utterly insignificant.

Cultivate, then, this pure and unselfish spirit, and combine with purity and faith, singleness of purpose, and you are evolving from within the elements, not only of abounding health and enduring success, but of **greatness** and power.

If your present position is distasteful to you, and your heart is not in your work, nevertheless perform your duties with scrupulous diligence, and whilst resting your mind in the idea that the better position and greater opportunities are waiting for you, ever keep an active mental outlook for budding possibilities, so that when the critical moment arrives, and the new channel presents itself, you will step into it with your mind fully prepared for the undertaking, and with that intelligence and foresight which is born of mental discipline.

Whatever your task may be, concentrate your whole mind upon it, throw into it all the energy of which you are capable. The faultless completion of small tasks leads inevitably to larger tasks. See to it that you rise by steady climbing, and you will never fall. And herein lies the secret of true power.

Learn, by constant practice, how to husband your resources, and to concentrate them, at any moment, upon a given point. The foolish waste all their mental and spiritual energy in frivolity, foolish chatter, or selfish argument, not to mention wasteful physical excesses.

If you would acquire overcoming power you must cultivate poise and passivity. You must be able to stand alone. All power is associated with immovability. The mountain, the massive rock, the storm-tried oak, all speak to us of power, because of their combined solitary grandeur and defiant fixity; while the shifting sand, the yielding twig, and the waving reed speak to us of weakness, because they are movable and non-resistant, and are utterly useless when detached from their fellows.

He is the man of power who, when all his fellows are swayed by some emotion or passion, remains calm and unmoved. He only is fitted to command and control who has succeeded in commanding and controlling himself.

The hysterical, the fearful, the thoughtless and frivolous, let such seek company, or they will fall for lack of support; but the calm, the fearless, the thoughtful, and let such seek the solitude of the forest, the desert, and the mountain-top, and to their power more power will be added, and they will more and more successfully stem the psychic currents and whirlpools which engulf mankind.

Passion is not power; it is the abuse of power, the dispersion of power. Passion is like a furious storm which beats fiercely and wildly upon the embattled rock whilst power is like the rock itself, which remains silent and unmoved through it all.

That was a manifestation of true power when Martin Luther, wearied with the persuasions of his fearful friends, who were doubtful as to his safety should he go to Worms, replied, "If there were as many devils in Worms as there are tiles on the housetops I would go."

And when Benjamin Disraeli broke down in his first Parliamentary speech, and brought upon himself the derision of the House, that was an exhibition of germinal power when he exclaimed, "The day will come when you will consider it an honor to listen to me."

When that young man, whom I knew, passing through continual reverses and misfortunes, was mocked by his friends and told to desist from further effort, and he replied, "The time is not far distant when you will marvel at my good fortune and success," he showed that he was possessed of that silent and irresistible power which has taken him over innumerable difficulties, and crowned his life with success.

If you have not this power, you may acquire it by practice, and the beginning of power is likewise the beginning of wisdom. You must commence by overcoming those purposeless trivialities to which you have hitherto been a willing victim.

Boisterous and uncontrolled laughter, slander and idle talk, and joking merely to raise a laugh, all these things must be put on one side as so much waste of valuable energy.

St. Paul never showed his wonderful insight into the hidden laws of human progress to greater advantage than when he warned the Ephesians against "Foolish talking and jesting which is not convenient," for to dwell habitually in such practices is to destroy all spiritual power and life.

As you succeed in rendering yourself impervious to such mental dissipations you will begin to understand what true power is, and you will then commence to grapple with the more powerful desires and appetites which hold your soul in bondage, and bar the way to power, and your further progress will then be made clear.

Above all be of single aim; have a legitimate and useful purpose, and devote yourself unreservedly to it. Let nothing draw you aside; remember that the double-minded man is unstable in all his ways.

Be eager to learn, but slow to beg. Have a thorough understanding of your work, and let it be your own; and as you proceed, ever following the inward Guide, the infallible Voice, you will pass on from victory to victory, and will rise step by step to higher resting-places, and your ever-broadening outlook will gradually reveal to you the essential beauty and purpose of life.

Self-purified, health will be yours; faith-protected, success will be yours; self-governed, power will be yours, and all that you do will prosper, for, ceasing to be a disjointed unit, self-enslaved, you will be in harmony with the Great Law, working no longer against, but with, the Universal Life, the Eternal Good.

And what health you gain it will remain with you; what success you achieve will be beyond all human computation, and will never pass away; and what influence and power you wield will continue to increase throughout the ages, for it will be a part of that unchangeable Principle which supports the universe.

This, then, is the secret of health,—a pure heart and a well-ordered mind; this is the secret of success,—an unfaltering faith, and a wisely-directed purpose; and to rein in, with unfaltering will, the dark steed of desire, this is the secret of power.

All ways are waiting for my feet to tread,
The light and dark, the living and the dead,
The broad and narrow way, the high and low,
The good and bad, and with quick step or slow,
I now may enter any way I will,
And find, by walking, which is good, which ill.

And all good things my wandering feet await,
If I but come, with vow inviolate,
Unto the narrow, high and holy way
Of heart-born purity, and therein stay;
Walking, secure from him who taunts and scorns,
To flowery meads, across the path of thorns.

And I may stand where health, success, and power
Await my coming, if, each fleeting hour,
I cling to love and patience; and abide
With stainlessness; and never step aside

From high integrity; so shall I see
At last the land of immortality.

And I may seek and find; I may achieve,
I may not claim, but, losing, may retrieve.
The law bends not for me, but I must bend
Unto the law, if I would reach the end
Of my afflictions, if I would restore
My soul to Light and Life, and weep no more.

Not mine the arrogant and selfish claim
To all good things; be mine the lowly aim
To seek and find, to know and comprehend,
And wisdom-ward all holy footsteps wend,
Nothing is mine to claim or to command,
But all is mine to know and understand

Chapter Six

THE SECRET OF ABOUNDING HAPPINESS

GREAT is the thirst for happiness, and equally great is the lack of happiness. The majority of the poor long for riches, believing that their possession would bring them supreme and lasting happiness.

Many who are rich, having gratified every desire and whim, suffer from ennui and repletion, and are farther from the possession of happiness even than the very poor.

If we reflect upon this state of things it will ultimately lead us to a knowledge of the all important truth that happiness is not derived from mere outward possessions, nor misery from the lack of them; for if this were so, we should find the poor always miserable, and the rich always happy, whereas the reverse is frequently the case.

Some of the most wretched people whom I have known were those who were surrounded with riches and luxury, whilst some of the brightest and happiest people I have met were possessed of only the barest necessities of life.

Many men who have accumulated riches have confessed that the selfish gratification which followed the acquisition of riches has robbed life of its sweetness, and that they were never so happy as when they were poor.

What, then, is happiness, and how is it to be secured? Is it a figment, a delusion, and is suffering alone perennial? We shall find, after earnest observation and reflection, that all, except those who have entered the way of wisdom, believe that happiness is only to be obtained by the gratification of desire.

It is this belief, rooted in the soil of ignorance, and continually watered by selfish cravings, that is the cause of all the misery in the world.

And I do not limit the word desire to the grosser animal cravings; it extends to the higher psychic realm, where far more powerful, subtle, and insidious cravings hold in bondage the intellectual and refined, depriving them of all that beauty, harmony, and purity of soul whose expression is happiness.

Most people will admit that selfishness is the cause of all the unhappiness in the world, but they fall under the soul-destroying delusion that it is somebody else's selfishness, and not their own.

When you are willing to admit that all your unhappiness is the result of your own selfishness you will not be far from the gates of Paradise; but so long as you are convinced that it is the selfishness of others that is robbing you of joy, so long will you remain a prisoner in your self-created purgatory.

Happiness is that inward state of perfect satisfaction which is joy and peace, and from which all desire is eliminated. The satisfaction which results from gratified desire is brief and illusionary, and is always followed by an increased demand for gratification.

Desire is as insatiable as the ocean, and clamors louder and louder as its demands are attended to.

It claims ever-increasing service from its deluded devotees, until at last they are struck down with physical or mental anguish, and are hurled into the purifying fires of suffering. Desire is the region of hell, and all torments are centered there.

The giving up of desire is the realization of heaven, and all delights await the pilgrim there,

> *I sent my soul through the invisible,*
> *Some letter of that after life to spell,*
> *And by-and-by my soul returned to me,*
> *And whispered, I myself am heaven and hell,"*

Heaven and hell are inward states. Sink into self and all its gratifications, and you sink into hell; rise above self into that state of consciousness which is the utter denial and forgetfulness of self, and you enter heaven.

Self is blind, without judgment, not possessed of true knowledge, and always leads to suffering. Correct perception, unbiased judgment, and true knowledge belong only to the divine state, and only in so far as you realize this divine consciousness can you know what real happiness is.

So long as you persist in selfishly seeking for your own personal happiness, so long will happiness elude you, and you will be sowing the seeds of wretchedness.

In so far as you succeed in losing yourself in the service of others, in that measure will happiness come to you, and you will reap a harvest of bliss.

> *It is in loving, not in being loved,*
> *The heart is blessed;*
> *It is in giving, not in seeking gifts,*
> *We find our quest.*

> *Whatever be thy longing or thy need,*
> *That do thou give;*
> *So shall thy soul be fed, and thou indeed*
> *Shalt truly live.*

Cling to self, and you cling to sorrow, relinquish self, and you enter into peace. To seek selfishly is not only to lose happiness, but even that which we believe to be the source of happiness.

See how the glutton is continually looking about for a new delicacy wherewith to stimulate his deadened appetite; and how, bloated, burdened, and diseased, scarcely any food at last is eaten with pleasure.

Whereas, he who has mastered his appetite, and not only does not seek, but never thinks of gustatory pleasure, finds delight in the most frugal meal. The angel-form of happiness, which men, looking through the eyes of self, imagine they see in gratified desire, when clasped is always found to be the skeleton of misery. Truly, "He that seeketh his life shall lose it, and he that loseth his life shall find it."

Abiding happiness will come to you when, ceasing to selfishly cling, you are willing to give up. When you are willing to lose, unreservedly, that impermanent thing which is so dear to you, and which, whether you cling to it or not, will one day be snatched from you, then you will find that that which seemed to you like a painful loss, turns out to be a supreme gain.

To give up in order to gain, than this there is no greater delusion, nor no more prolific source of misery; but to be willing to yield up and to suffer loss, this is indeed the Way of Life.

How is it possible to find real happiness by centering ourselves in those things which, by their very nature, must pass away? Abiding and real happiness can only be found by centering ourselves in that which is permanent.

Rise, therefore, above the clinging to and the craving for impermanent things, and you will then enter into a consciousness of the Eternal, and as, rising above self, and by growing more and more into the spirit of purity, self-sacrifice and universal Love, you become centered in that consciousness, you will realize that happiness which has no reaction, and which can never be taken from you.

The heart that has reached utter self-forgetfulness in its love for others has not only become possessed of the highest happiness but has entered into immortality, for it has realized the Divine.

Look back upon your life, and you will find that the moments of supremest happiness were those in which you uttered some word, or performed some act, of compassion or self-denying love. Spiritually, happiness and harmony are, synonymous.

Harmony is one phase of the Great Law whose spiritual expression is love. All selfishness is discord, and to be selfish is to be out of harmony with the Divine order.

As we realize that all-embracing love which is the negation of self, we put ourselves in harmony with the divine music, the universal song, and that ineffable melody which is true happiness becomes our own.

Men and women are rushing hither and thither in the blind search for happiness, and cannot find it; nor ever will until they recognize that happiness is already within them and round about them, filling the universe, and that they, in their selfish searching are shutting themselves out from it.

I followed happiness to make her mine,
Past towering oak and swinging ivy vine.
She fled, I chased, o'er slanting hill and dale,
O'er fields and meadows, in the purpling vale;
Pursuing rapidly o'er dashing stream.
I scaled the dizzy cliffs where eagles scream;
I traversed swiftly every land and M.
But always happiness eluded me.

Exhausted, fainting, I pursued no more,
But sank to rest upon a barren shore.
One came and asked for food, and one for alms
I placed the bread and gold in bony palms.
One came for sympathy, and one for rest;
I shared with every needy one my best;
When, lo! sweet Happiness, with form divine,
Stood by me, whispering softly, 'I am thine'.

These beautiful lines of Burleigh's express the secret of all
abounding happiness. Sacrifice the personal and transient, and
you rise at once into the impersonal and permanent.

Give up that narrow cramped self that seeks to render all things subservient to its own petty interests, and you will enter into the company of the angels, into the very heart and essence of universal Love.

Forget yourself entirely in the sorrows of others and in ministering to others, and divine happiness will emancipate you from all sorrow and suffering.

"Taking the first step with a good thought, the second with a good word, and the third with a good deed, I entered Paradise." And you also may enter into Paradise by pursuing the same course. It is not beyond, it is here. It is realized only by the unselfish.

It is known in its fullness only to the pure in heart. If you have not realized this unbounded happiness you may begin to actualize it by ever holding before you the lofty ideal of unselfish love, and aspiring towards it.

Aspiration or prayer is desire turned upward. It is the soul turning toward its Divine source, where alone permanent satisfaction can be found. By aspiration the destructive forces of desire are transmuted into divine and all-preserving energy.

To aspire is to make an effort to shake off the trammels of desire; it is the prodigal made wise by loneliness and suffering, returning to his Father's Mansion.

As you rise above the sordid self; as you break, one after another, the chains that bind you, will you realize the joy of giving, as distinguished from the misery of grasping - giving of your substance; giving of your intellect; giving of the love and light that is growing within you.

You will then understand that it is indeed "more blessed to give than to receive."

But the giving must be of the heart without any taint of self, without desire for reward. The gift of pure love is always attended with bliss. If, after you have given, you are wounded because you are not thanked or flattered, or your name put in the paper, know then that your gift was prompted by vanity and not by love, and you were merely giving in order to get; were not really giving, but grasping.

Lose yourself in the welfare of others; forget yourself in all that you do; this is the secret of abounding happiness.

Ever be on the watch to guard against selfishness, and learn faithfully the divine lessons of inward sacrifice; so shall you climb the highest heights of happiness, and shall remain in the neverclouded sunshine of universal joy, clothed in the shining garment of immortality.

Are you searching for the happiness that does not fade away?

Are you looking for the joy that lives, and leaves no grievous day?

Are you panting for the waterbrooks of Love, and Life, and Peace?

Then let all dark desires depart, and selfish seeking cease.

Are you ling'ring in the paths of pain, grief-haunted, stricken sore?

Are you wand'ring in the ways that wound your weary feet
the more?

Are you sighing for the Resting-Place where tears and sorrows
cease?

Then sacrifice your selfish heart and find the Heart of Peace.

Chapter Seven

THE REALIZATION OF PROSPERITY

It is granted only to the heart that abounds with integrity, trust, generosity and love to realize true prosperity. The heart that is not possessed of these qualities cannot know prosperity, for prosperity, like happiness, is not an outward possession, but an inward realization.

The greedy man may become a millionaire, but he will always be wretched, and mean, and poor, and will even consider himself outwardly poor so long as there is a man in the world who is richer than himself, whilst the upright, the open-handed and loving will realize a full and rich prosperity, even though their outward possessions may be small.

He is poor who is dissatisfied; he is rich who is contented with what he has, and he is richer who is generous with what he has.

When we contemplate the fact that the universe is abounding in all good things, material as well as spiritual, and compare it with man's blind eagerness to secure a few gold coins, or a few acres of dirt, it is then that we realize how dark and ignorant selfishness is; it is then that we know that self-seeking is self-destruction.

Nature gives all, without reservation, and loses nothing; man, grasping all, loses everything.

If you would realize true prosperity do not settle down, as many have done, into the belief that if you do right everything will go wrong. Do not allow the word "competition" to shake your faith in the supremacy of righteousness.

I care not what men may say about the "laws of competition," for do I not know the unchangeable Law, which shall one day put them all to rout, and which puts them to rout even now in the heart and life of the righteous man?

And knowing this Law I can contemplate all dishonesty with undisturbed repose, for I know where certain destruction awaits it. Under all circumstances do that which you believe to be right, and trust the Law; trust the Divine Power that is imminent in the universe, and it will never desert you, and you will always be protected.

By such a trust all your losses will be converted into gains, and all curses which threaten will be transmuted into blessings. Never let go of integrity, generosity, and love, for these, coupled with energy, will lift you into the truly prosperous state.

Do not believe the world when it tells you that you must always attend to "number one" first, and to others afterwards. To do this is not to think of others at all, but only of one's own comforts.

To those who practice this the day will come when they will be deserted by all, and when they cry out in their loneliness and anguish there will be no one to hear and help them. To consider one's self before all others is to cramp and warp and hinder every noble and divine impulse.

Let your soul expand, let your heart reach out to others in loving and generous warmth, and great and lasting will be your joy, and all prosperity will come to you. Those who have wandered from the highway of righteousness guard themselves against competition; those who always pursue the right need not to trouble about such defense.

This is no empty statement, There are men today who, by the power of integrity and faith, have defied all competition, and who, without swerving in the least from their methods, when competed with, have risen steadily into prosperity, whilst those who tried to undermine them have fallen back defeated.

To possess those inward qualities which constitute goodness is to be armored against all the powers of evil, and to be doubly protected in every time of trial; and to build' oneself up in those qualities is to build up a success which cannot be shaken, and to enter into a prosperity which will endure forever.

> *The White Robe of the Heart Invisible*
> *Is stained with sin and sorrow, grief and pain,*
> *And all repentant pools and springs of prayer*
> *Shall not avail to wash it white again.*
>
> *While in the path of ignorance I walk,*
> *The stains of error will not cease to cling*
> *Defilements mark the crooked path of self,*
> *Where anguish lurks and disappointments sting.*
>
> *Knowledge and wisdom only can avail*
> *To purify and make my garment clean,*
> *For therein lie love's waters; therein rests*
> *Peace undisturbed, eternal, and serene.*
>
> *Sin and repentance is the path of pain,*
> *Knowledge and wisdom is the path of Peace*
> *By the near way of practice I will find*
> *Where bliss begins, how pains and sorrows cease.*
>
> *Self shall depart, and Truth shall take its place*
> *The Changeless One, the Indivisible*
> *Shall take up His abode in me, and cleanse*
> *The White Robe of the Heart Invisible.*

Chapters

1, 14 + 7

every day for 30 days